Published by Eastern Heroes Publishing
Produced by Rick Baker

Design & layout: Tim Hollingsworth
Instagram: 79_design

Printing: Ingramspark

Contributors:

UK
Rick Baker, Michael Nesbitt, Johnny Burnett, Simon Pritchard, Jason McNeil

USA
Hector Martinez
John Negron

GERMANY
Thomas Gross

Special Thanks
Thank you to John Negron for taking the time out to showcase his fabulous collection, the inspiration for this issue

All rights reserved. No part of this publication may be reproduced or transmitted in any or by any means, graphic, electronic or mechanical, including photocopying, recording, taping or any information storage and retrieval system, without prior written permission of the publisher.
© 2021 Eastern Heroes.

Editorial

Issue No.3 already! But this issue we have made it a Green Hornet Special! I would like to thank my good friend John Negron who inspired this issue by allowing me to showcase a large part of his fantastic Green Hornet collection, a must for Bruce Lee memorabilia collectors.
John's Bruce Lee collection is one of the most comprehensive I have seen and I was grateful that he allowed the readers to enjoy his many years of collecting. I hope to do more features in his extensive collection in future issues. Also thank you to Thomas Gross for sharing his collection of rare lobby card sand posters, making this another bumper issue. Time now to get back to work on The Game of Death redux 2.0 edition which looks at film maker Alan Canvan's three year journey bringing you the most complete cut of the pagoda ending.

Thank you all again for your support.

Keep the faith.

Rick Baker

Contents

4. Exploring the sting
11. Black Beauty Restoration
22. Autograph collection
32. Robin Vs Kato
34. The long strange trip
38. Screen test
44. The great Green Hornet find
46. Memorabilia section
70. The German collector
96. 5 Fingers of discs

EXPLORING THE STING! OF THE GREEN HORNET

By John Negron

Bruce Lee's Legacy continues to reach new heights year after year, always spreading to new shores being that we just celebrated what would have been Bruce Lee's 81st Birthday. The legacy he left behind has not let up one bit in 48 years! There are still countless books, Magazines, JKD schools, Countless articles, Novelty Items, Statues, stamps anything and everything you can imagine still being produced and highly sought after by collector's and fans all over the world. Sometimes it feels as if we just lost this great Icon of the 20th Century. Magazines and advertisers use his likeness more and more each day. The more items that come out the more fans want. But taking a step back when we talk about Bruce Lee's early beginnings in the late 60's or his early introduction to a widespread audience, we can't help but remember him as Kato the Green Hornets valet in the 1966 T.V series. I have written many articles for different publications in the past but sitting here thinking on what I wanted to contribute to this great Magazine that has not already been talked about countless times? And then it hit me I would like to do an article covering the Green Hornet and some of its roots before Bruce and how he became known in Japan for his role that was referred to as "The Kato Show". Being a very significant part of Bruce's rise to stardom in my opinion, this was our first introduction of "Gung-Fu" as he described it in that Iconic Black & White screen test and in that famous vintage highly sought after First cover appearance in the 1967 Black Belt Magazine. Many times, we have heard that Bruce did not like his work on the Green Hornet but to me that was his early beginnings and gave us a first introduction to Bruce Lee and his "Gung-Fu". But for die hard Green Hornet Fans what a treat from Radio to serials to the small screens into our homes in 1966! Although the show lasted 1 season and 26 episodes because everyone seemed to be watching the campy Batman T.V series and not the seriously played opposite the Green Hornet. Perhaps doing this period Campy was in instead of serious, who knows but what we do know is there was nothing else at that time that showed fists and feet flying around and there it started WHO WAS THIS GUY??? Well, we found out pretty quick that the veteran actor playing the Green Hornet was Van Williams and the guy whizzing around was none other than Bruce Lee! Let's not forget the rolling arsenal the Black Beauty. I would briefly like to take on the collecting and merchandising aspect of the show the 1st episode titled "The Silent Gun" aired on September 9,1966 on ABC Television, Batman was already enjoying the success of numerous toys and Batman was in full swing as far as toys were concerned. The Green Hornet toys & merchandise were only being produced on the East Coast as I have been told by a world renown very prominent Green Hornet Collector Perry Lee the toys according to Perry were not distributed on the West Coast in the United States. He also has stated that very few companies compared to Batman were producing Green Hornet Memorabilia and it seems that by the time the merchandise started coming out the show had already been cancelled. As rare as the GH merchandise is I don't think since the show was cancelled by the time the items hit the streets that the items were mass produced hence the really high prices for GH items especially since the show aired some 55 years ago and the memorabilia falls into several different collector's categories. what I would like to do here is share some facts on the Green Hornet as I am fascinated with the history of not only the 1966 T.V show but the background of this character and a little about its history & origins. Here are some very interesting facts about the Green Hornet.

Fact # 1 - The Green Hornet radio show was a collaboration of 2 men George Washington Trendle & Fran Striker at the Mutual Building in Downtown Detroit back in 1936 and was launched on Radio station WXYZ in 1936.

Fact # 2 - George Trendle & Fran Striker developed 3 different characters. One was the Lone Ranger who was the great uncle of the G.H The second was Sergeant Preston of the Yukon and the Third of course being the Green Hornet.

Fact # 3 - Each of the characters that were developed by George & Fran had their own overviews according to interviews with Mr. Trendle they were as follows: The Lone Ranger was created with the following premise to teach youngsters respect for the law. Sergeant Preston of the Yukon's premise was to teach teenagers the love of country and animals. The Green Hornet however according to George was created to appeal to an older group. Mr. Trendle was quoted as saying " That he wanted to show that racketeers and crooked politicians could succeed unless they were stopped" According to source books on the history of the G.H Mr. Trendle believed that the G.H was THE BEST of the 3 characters mentioned.

Fact # 4 - In 1939 Gordon Jones played the role of the Green Hornet and Keye Luke played the role of Kato in a 15-part serial (Keye Luke as you may recall played the blind shaolin monk in the 70's T.V series Kung Fu.

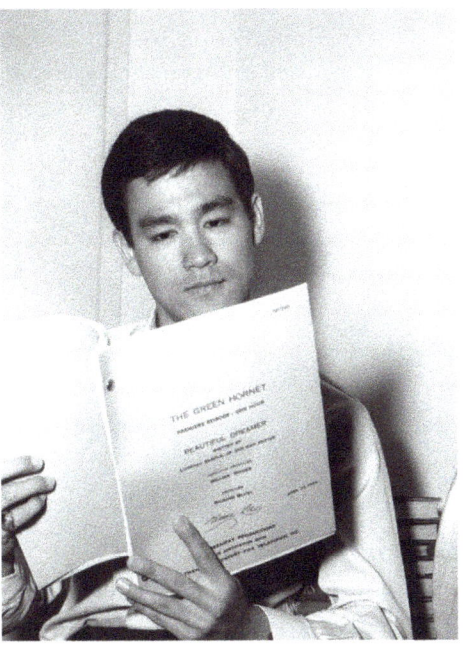

Fact # 5 - 1940-1949 Harvey Comics launched a 64-page comic book " The Green Hornet" as their comic Book hero.

Fact # 6 – In 1949 one of the earliest pieces of Hornet merchandise came when the Golden Jersey Milk company offered customers a chance to own drinking glasses emblazoned with images of the characters that were in the series (These are very rare sought-after pieces to the modern-day G.H collector of today and I have yet to own this rare piece among others)

Fact # 7 – The better little book company produced printed text adventures and General Mills a breakfast cereal company special G.H cereal boxes which had "the Green Hornet's amazing model city buildings" printed on the backs of small variety packs along with cut out vehicles including the Black Beauty.

Fact # 8 – During the 1950's when the Radio series had been cancelled and the comic book ceased publication the character of the Green Hornet had become forgotten or did it??

George Trendle was very difficult to work with as far as bringing his vision of the Green Hornet to T.V screens. Once things went back and forth and different things were agreed on mostly money issues also George was instrumental in saying how he wanted his character portrayed he went on to tell William Dozier that he that he had assisted in the production of over 3,000 Lone Ranger radio shows and some 2,000 Sergeant Preston of the Yukon radio shows and more than 400 Green Hornet radio shows he stressed to them that "he knew a thing or two about the industry and what the audiences liked" There were certain things that were being written for the show but there were things that George would not bend on from the radio show such as preserving the "Flight of the Bumble Bee theme", the secret panel that led to a hidden stairway, anti-racketeering theme that murder was only to be an incidental occurrence he felt the show should be aimed at the young voters of America and to teach them how to avoid being taken by rackets and crooked politicians. As you see the history of the Green Hornet and how it came to be all the way back into the early days are very fascinating to read about and then to see what we finally were given in 1966 hence my big fascination with the Green Hornet character. To continue how difficult George Trendle was being he had more demands such as the city, the car, the way Scanlon

once again was comparing these differences to the current Batman character. Without making this article long and drawn out Trendle continued to be difficult on how he wanted the music score, Characters portrayals in the series as close to the radio show and on and on. It got to a point where he was told that no one was going to notice these details because there was no one in the age group that would remember the old radio shows. Now remember fans George Trendle was at this time in 1966 in his early 80's. One excellent thing that came from George was that he loved Bruce Lee as Kato from his screen test and well we will see history develop for our guy. What's funny here is Trendle wanted a sort of hanging

was to be a commissioner, Britt Reid's Father was to be alive and visit like in the radio Broadcast. Trendle was upset that he imagined that his character was going to be portrayed like their current character of "Batman" and let's not even visit the Black Beauty Trendle wanted the Green Hornet and Kato to wear just cloth type mask's that hung down from the nose and opera capes. But did it end here no Trendle had a vision for his character and continued to be very precise on what he expected it to be portrayed like he did not like that Scanlon was entering to see Britt through some secret passageway, because this was a Batman series attempt. Trendle was so picky that he even changed how Mike Axford was to address Lenore Case the secretary, he wanted Mike to call her by "Casey" and Britt was to address her by Miss Case. He wanted the car to look like any other car and not necessarily a car that would be associated with the Green Hornet. Trendle also had a problem with the revolving personal car of Britt to the Black Beauty he wanted simplicity such as an elevator. He

cloth mask and while still arguing. The cast was already being picked for Britt, Kato,

Scanlon and Axford by this point its about May 1966. Ironically The original character who was Al Hodge contacted several people to be involved in behind the scenes and suggested that Cato be changed to Kato as the story has it, he was declined to work on the series. In continuing to keep Trendle in the loop on things he wanted to be informed of the approval of the cast he loved the casting of Walter Brooke as Scanlon from the start said he fit the role perfectly but he was not very pleased with Casey or Axford he wanted Axford's role to be a cracker jack reporter but bumbling and the actress that was originally looked at for Casey was a no go her name was Lynn Borden a blonde. As you can see from the series a beautiful redhead named Wende Wagner was chosen. It seems that Trendle all the way until actual filming was to be begin was still harping on the entrance through the fireplace of Scanlon, and the relationship of Axford. On September 9, 1966, the Green Hornet debuted beating out football on NBC and a Wild, Wild West repeat on CBS! The show was not received well by the local Detroit press who were expecting by all the publicity leading to the debut to be more like Batman. But again, it was stressed this was a serious character. Early on some of the reviews put Kato to be the real hero of the show! After viewing the show and with the ratings being favorable Trendle wanted some changes he wanted less of Scanlon, a more personable Green Hornet, and more Gung Fu in lighted areas! The show was cancelled after 26 episodes. With episode #26 Airing March 17, 1967 The Most interesting thing is what the actor's what paid on the Green

Hornet series Van Williams $2,000 Bruce Lee $400-550 depending on the episode, Wende Wagner $850, Walter Brooke $750, Lloyd Gough $1,000, These were the standard salaries but could go up a little depending on the episodes which had different production costs. One interesting note is on Jan 27, 1967, to Feb 3, 1967, a two-part presentation was made "A Piece of the Action" & "Batman's Satisfaction" Van Williams & Bruce Lee were not paid the same amount as the other GH stars Van received $1,250 per episode instead of $2,000 and Bruce $375 instead of $550.

It is believed that this was a rushed deal to try and promote the GH who was facing cancellation and hoping to acquire the fans of the Batman series by doing a cross-over as you may have guessed this did not sit well with Trendle. On Jan 3, 1967, William Dozier gave George Trendle the bad news that the series was not being renewed. What we must try to understand here is that Batman had a strong appeal to kids through Comic books and the green hornet was a radio series drama. Had the GH been given a 1-hour time slot and deeper story lines I believe it would have survived in the long run. Now to collectibles…. I will do my best to account for some of the rarest green hornet items that exist or that I have seen in either my collection or in collections of very prominent GH collector's that I know have some of the world's top GH collections there are only two which come to mind and those two collectors are Mr. Perry Lee and Frank Romero I base this from the very rare items I have seen that they possess. So let's start with the early collectibles dating back and moving forward:

Here are some of the Licensees and the merchandise they produced:
Western Publishing & Lithographing Co.- Various publications, Inlay puzzles, coloring books, comic books and other paper items. Milton Bradley Co.- Games & Boxed Puzzles. Donrusss Co.-Trading cards with bubble Gum Aurora Plastics Corp- Hobby & Slot car kits. The Mermaid Corp - Bibs Norwich Mills- Sweatshirts, t-shirts, Pajamas Ed-U-Cards – Playing cards Colorforms- Signal Light, Print putty, Stick ons. Green Duck Co. - Buttons Shapiro and Sons- Bedspreads, Curtains Folz Vending Co. – Charms for vending machines. Perfect fit industries- Towels, Quilts, Rugs Mattoy Playcraft, LTD- Corgi Collector cars. Arlington Hat Co.- Hats, Masks Jama Rama- Cut & Sew Pajamas Ben Cooper, Inc- masquerade costumes, Playsuits Opti-Ray Sunglasses- Sunglasses BZ Industries- Ready to Race Slot Cars S. Goldberg – House slippers. Mobile-O Enterprises- Three-dimensional paper puppets. Kayser-Roth – Hosiery, Fabric Headbands. Mattel Inc.- cars, Guns, vinyl products like wallets, cases, etc... The federal Glass Co. – Glassware.
Oak Rubber Co. – Vinyl & Rubber Balls Topps Chewing Gum – Pressure-Sensitive Stickers King-Seeley Thermos Co. – Lunch Kits, Thermos Bottles Roalex – Kites, Sliding Square Puzzles Ideal Toy Corp.

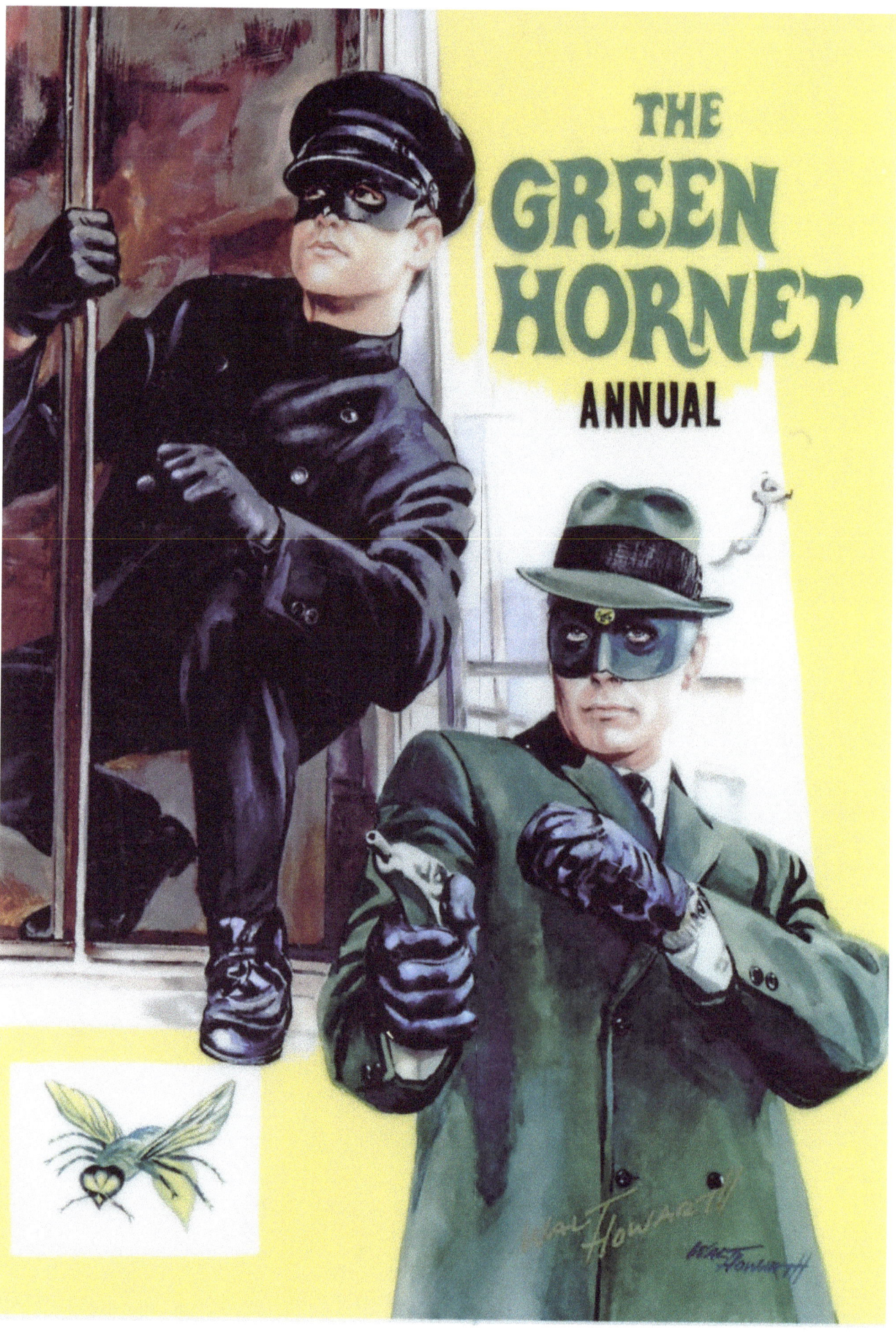

– hand Puppets, Inflatables, Play outfits Gower Printing – Water Decals, Stickers Lakeside Industries- Flexible Figure Trans World Sales – Plastic Mugs and Tumblers. Kenilworth Sportwear Inc. – Boys & Girls slacks, Shorts & Crawlers Perfect Fit Industries Inc. – Linen Hanging Towel, Bath Towels, Beach Towels, wash Cloths, and patchwork quilts Al Fischer and Co. -Black beauty coin operated Kiddy ride (The rarest GH item in existence). Ideal Toy- Captain Action Records/Music The Horn Meets the Hornet/ Al Hirt cover with the Green Hornet RCA Victor 1966 The Green Hornet Original Television Score Record Album, Composed by Billy May/Show Hornet Logo on Cover 20th Century Fox Records 1966. Green Hornet still at Large Record Album with Cover of Green Hornet & Kato Nostalgia Lane Inc. The Official Adventures of the Green Hornet Record Album Cover photo of Green Hornet & Kato/MGM Leo the Lion Records.

The Better Little Books- 1940's standard size of these three books 1940/The Green Hornet Strikes, 1941/The Green Hornet Returns, 1942/The Green Hornet Cracks Down is 3 5/8 inches by 4 ½ inches and 1 ½ inches thick 432 pages. An estimated 10,000 copies of these 2 books were printed. These are HIGHLY sought after and impossible to find in MINT condition now because of age. The Helnit Publishing Company- Comic appearances of the Green Hornet Issue # 1 Dec 1940-issue # 47 1949. Harvey One-time shots- Character appeared in various comics for various reasons such as war bonds 1942, and crime story's 1947, etc. Four Color Comics- September 1953 Trendle's attempt to rekindle interest two stories were featured. Gold Key Comics- All 3 had beautiful Van Williams & Bruce Lee GH/Kato Covers also highly sought after by GH/Bruce Lee and comic book collector's/3 issues first two were one story and the third was a 2 story with a 12 cents price. Issue 1 released Feb 1967 "Ring of Terror", Issue 2 released May 1967 "The Threat of the Red Dragons" Issue 3 Released August 1967 "The Counterplot Affair"/" Masquerade" TV Tornado – #12 published a 2-page comic strip called "assassins" in England April 1967. The Now Comics- Premiere issue November 1989/Final issue no.14 in late 1990 Excellent Comic Book series but Tony Caputo was believed to have money problems and caused the comic series to go under. The first 12 issues were collected into one big hardcover book that featured an introduction by Van Williams and was released in 1990. These I was told were discontinued due to not receiving permissions from Now Comics?

The Sting of the Green Hornet- released from Jun-Sep 1992 4 issues. These were considered BIG fan favorites.

The Green Hornet continues- Now comics return (1991-1995) about 40 comics. To increase sales and popularity collectibles were inserted in certain issues such as posters, Buttons, hologram trading cards,

Tales of the Green Hornet- 1990 Now comics spin off 9 issues. Van Williams wrote the stories for the 1st two issues! These are believed to be tributes written for Bruce Lee "Five fists of the Dragon" & Flashing Fingers of Death" Quick Note noted author James Van Hise also got on board for the remaining 7 issues released in 1992 also for the miniseries Solitary Sentinel (1992-1993)

The Green Hornet Dark Tomorrow- 3 issues 1993 Kato Miniseries- Now Comics 1991-1992 after this Now finally came to an end again supposedly because of Caputo again mismanaging his money killed the almost 100 issue series.

There has been other comic book series by Dynamite Comics and others, but the ones mentioned above are the most notable. We cannot mention the Green Hornet without mention of the 2011 Movie that starred Seth Rogan as GH and Jay Chou as Kato. Although I am thankful for trying to keep the GH alive the movie was considered a disaster because they had the opportunity for the character of Britt Reid to turn around but instead, they opted to keep selling Rogan's cheap shots and jokes. Jay Chou did an outstanding job at Kato, and I was hoping that the movie would do for the Green Hornet what Michael Keaton did for Batman but instead we were highly disappointed. Now we fans await for Hollywood to remake and release another Green hornet movie and do it the justice it deserves and one day we hopefully we might see the Green Hornet T.V series done in a Blu Ray release hopefully.

THE RESTORATION AND CREATION OF THE GREEN HORNET'S BLACK BEAUTY
PHOTO GALLERY

The Green Hornet television show of 1966/67 with Van Williams as the Hornet and his co-star Bruce Lee as the stinger, two Black Beauties were built by star Hollywood carmaker Dean Jeffries, both based on 1966 Imperials, here we show in photographs how this epic transformation evolved to one of the best known on screen TV cars.

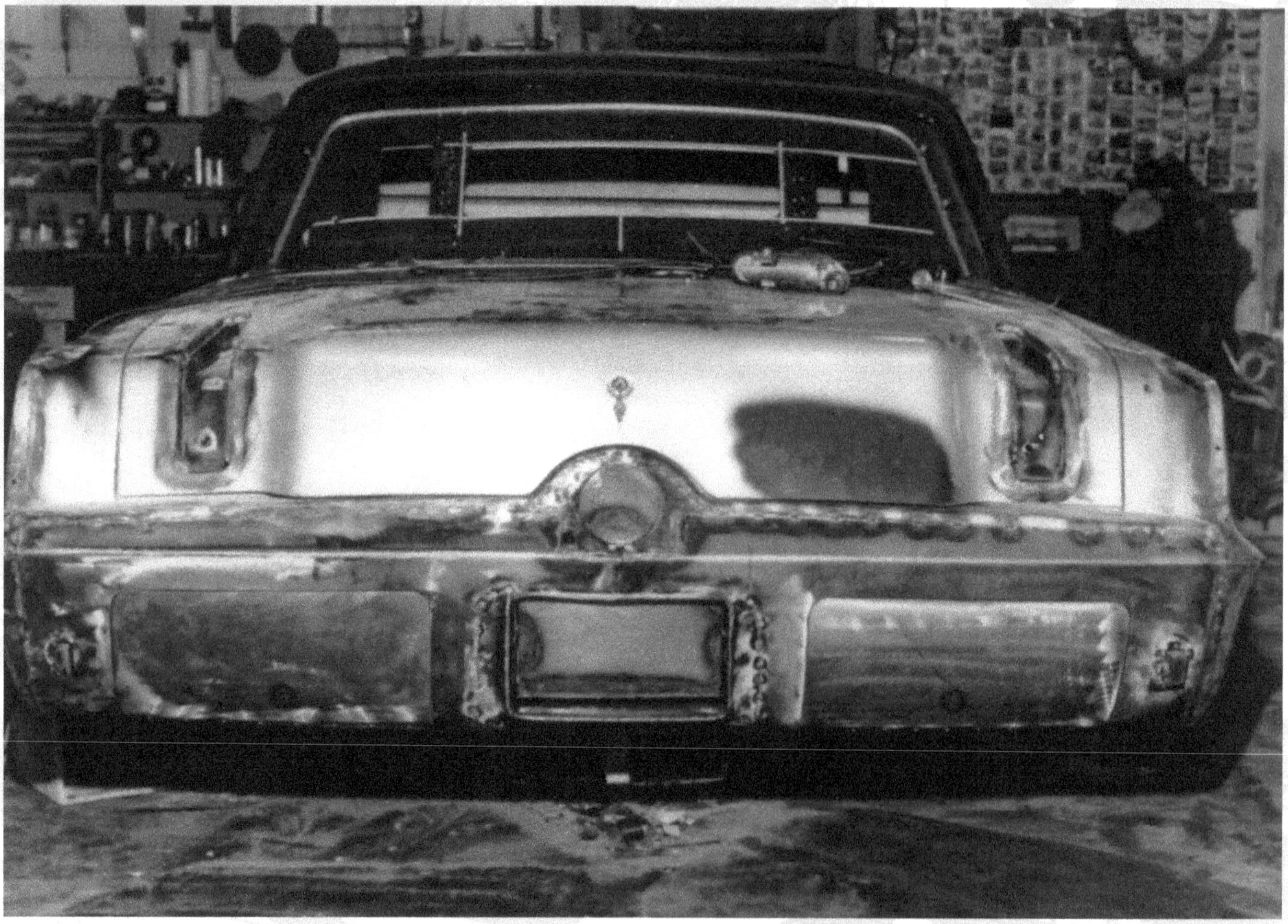

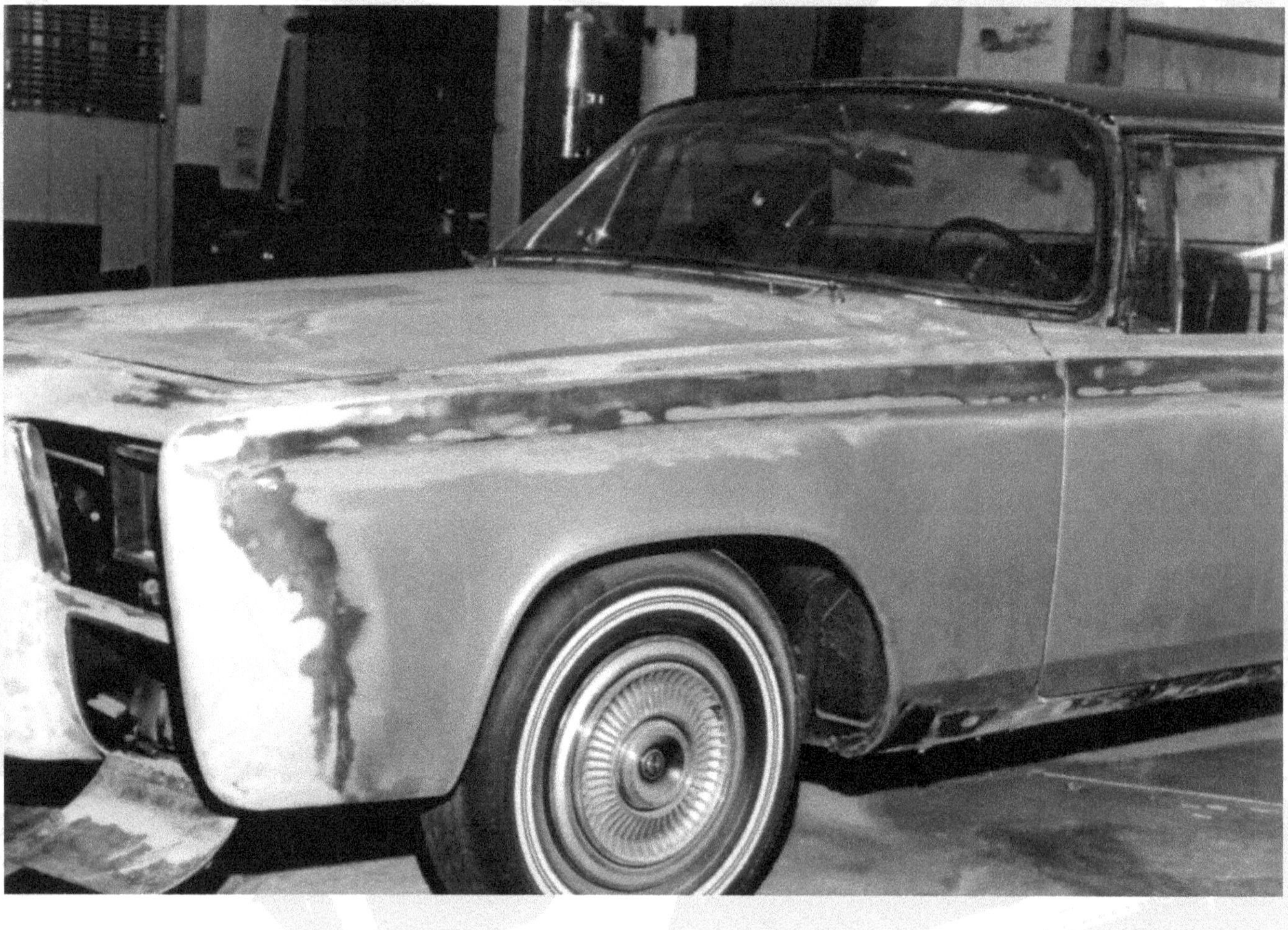

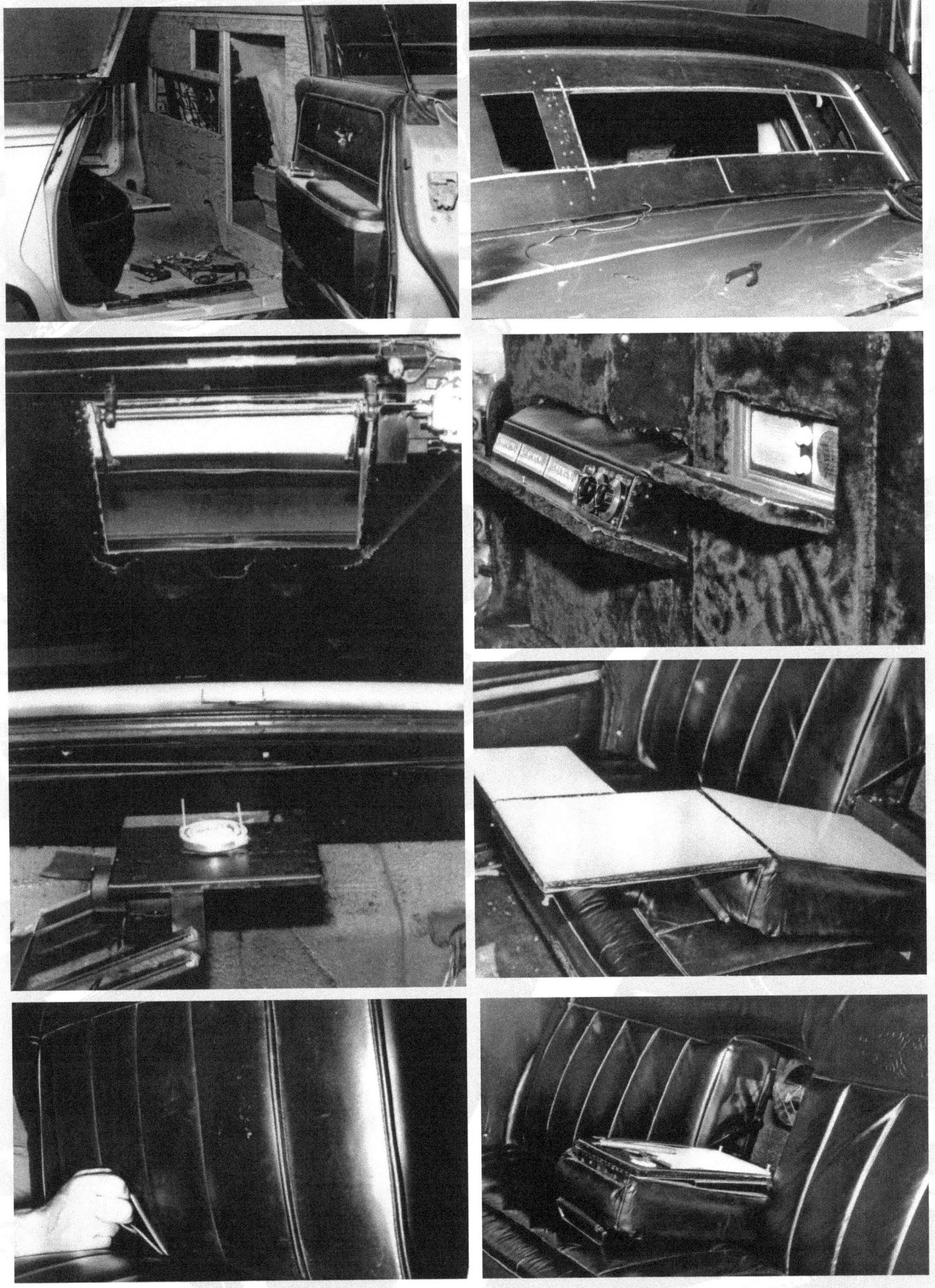

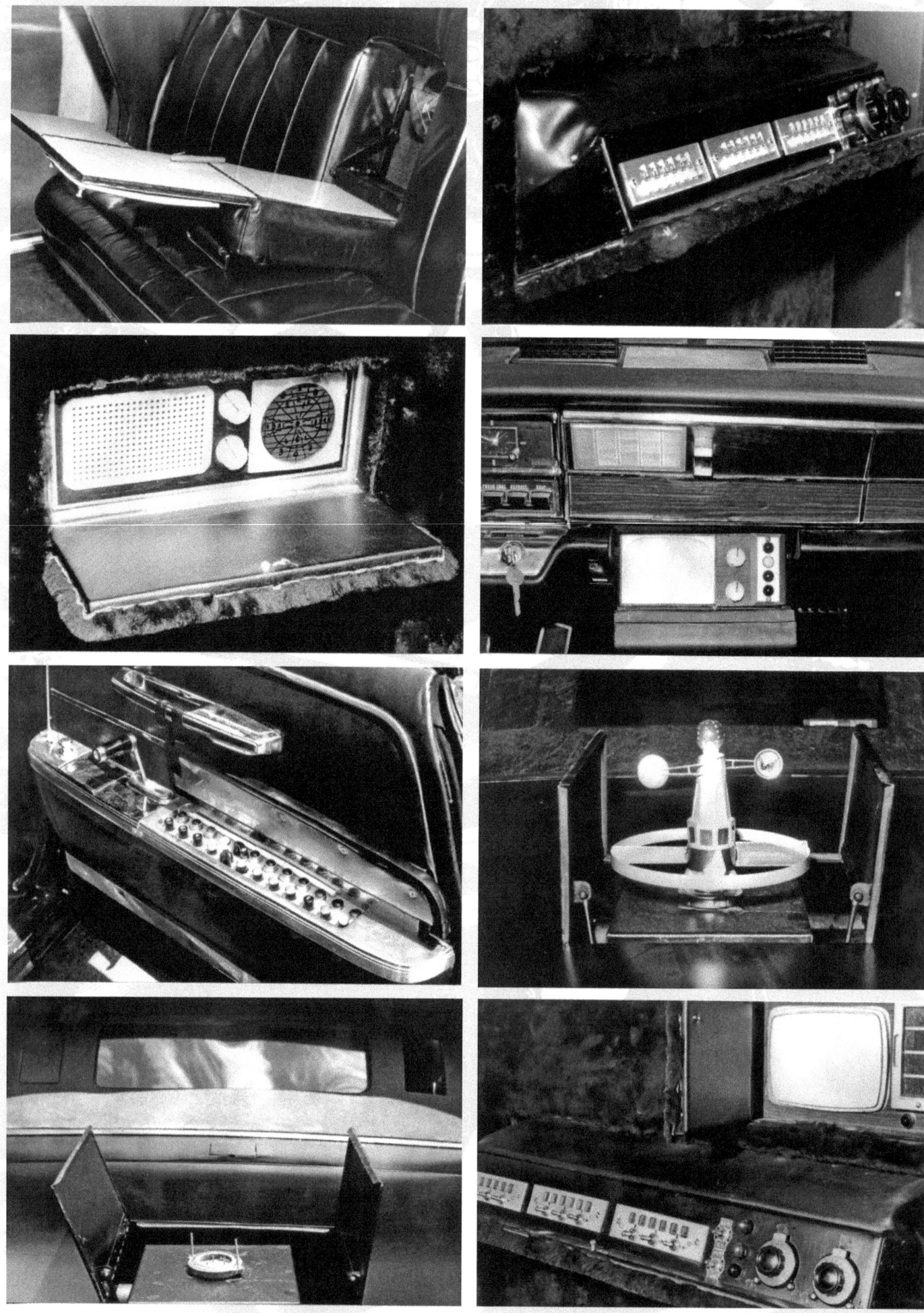

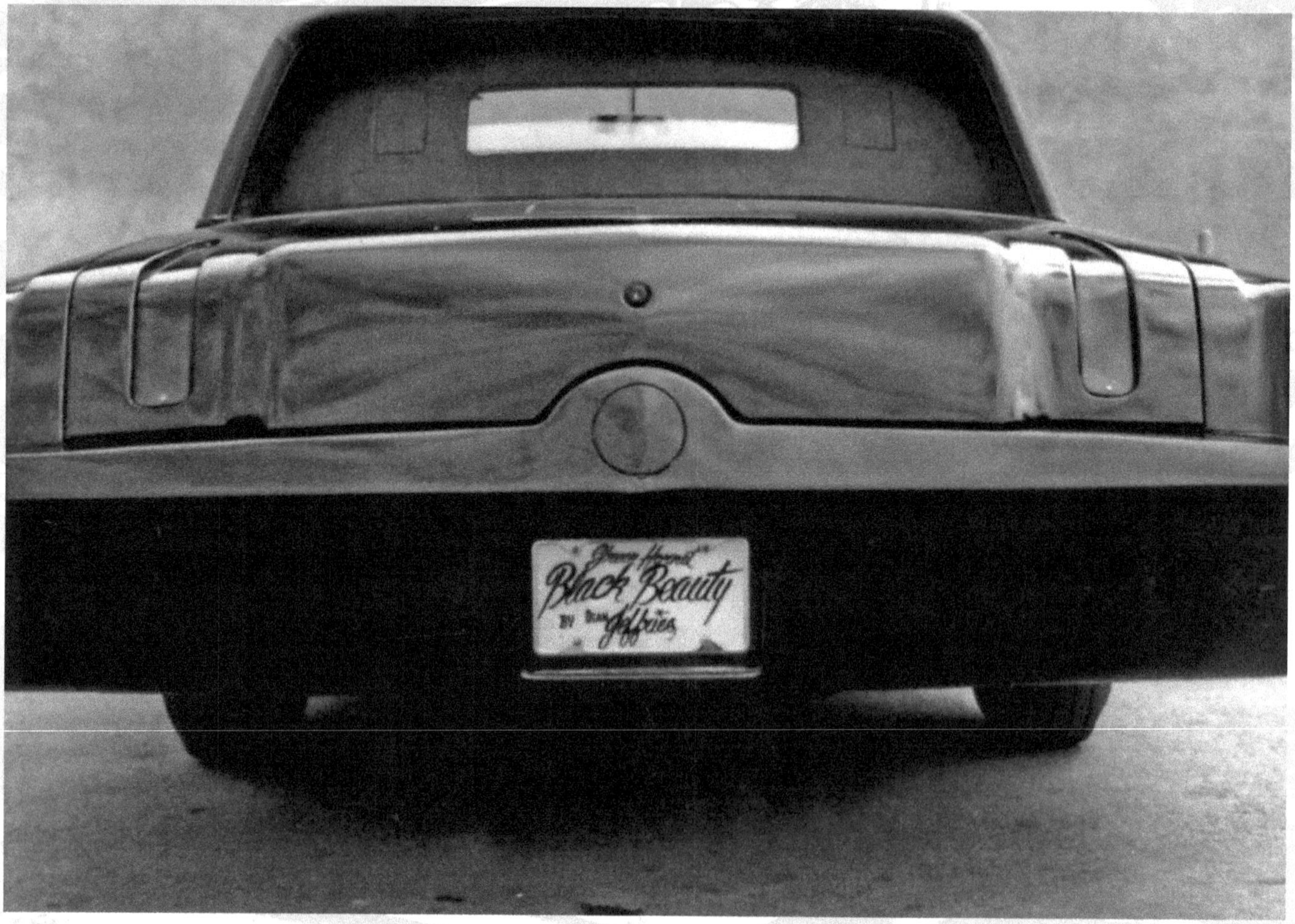
Black Beauty

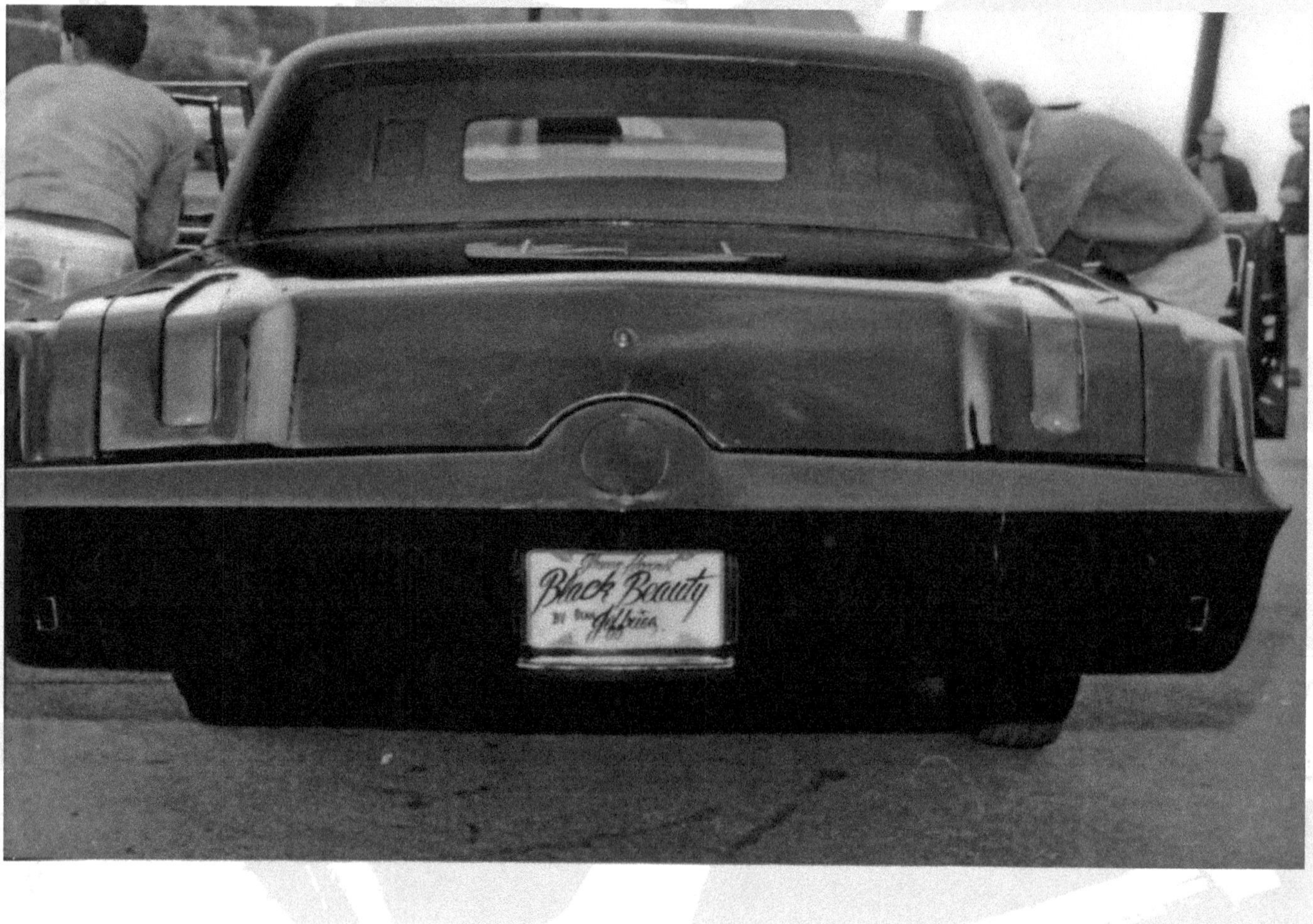
Black Beauty

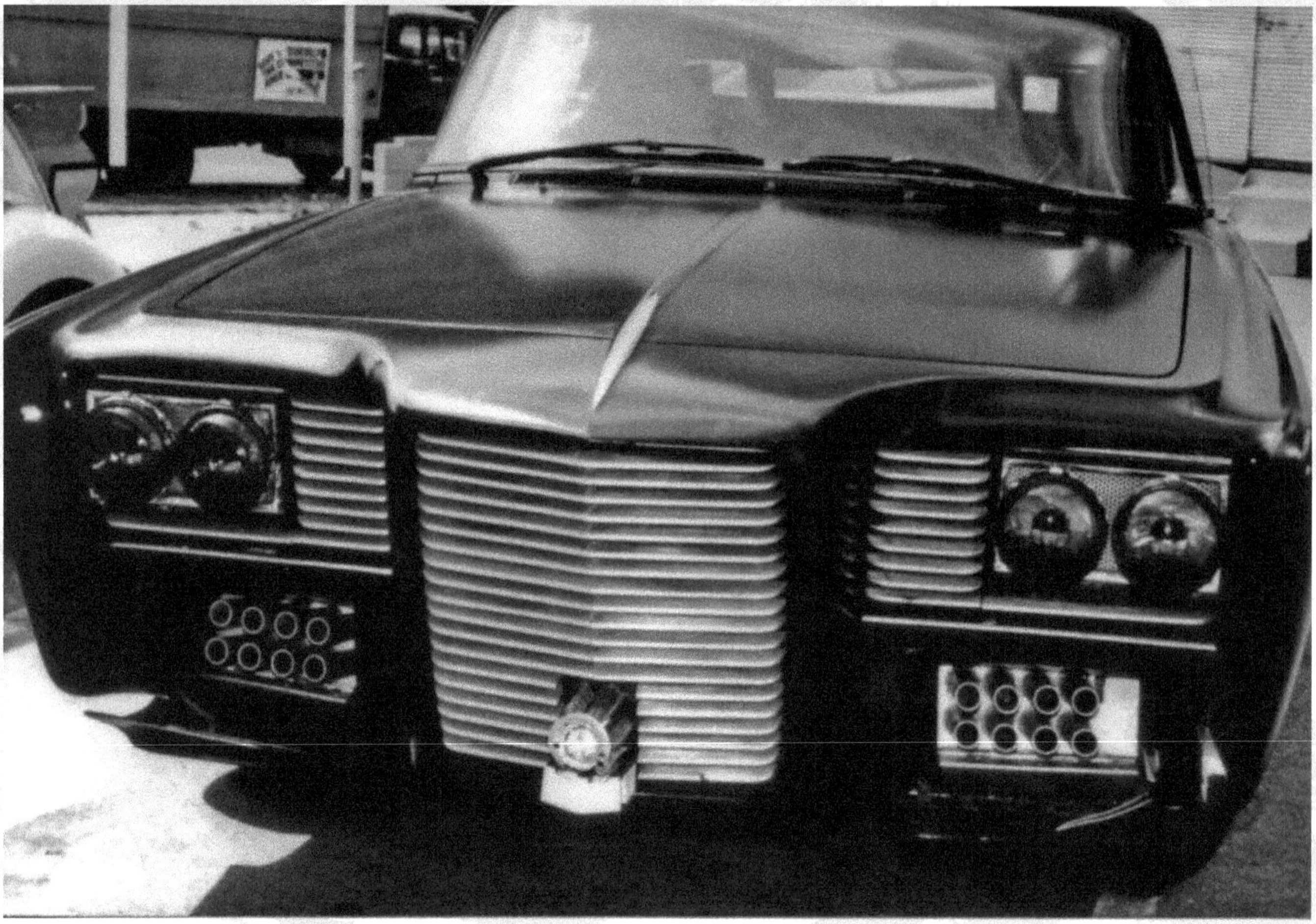

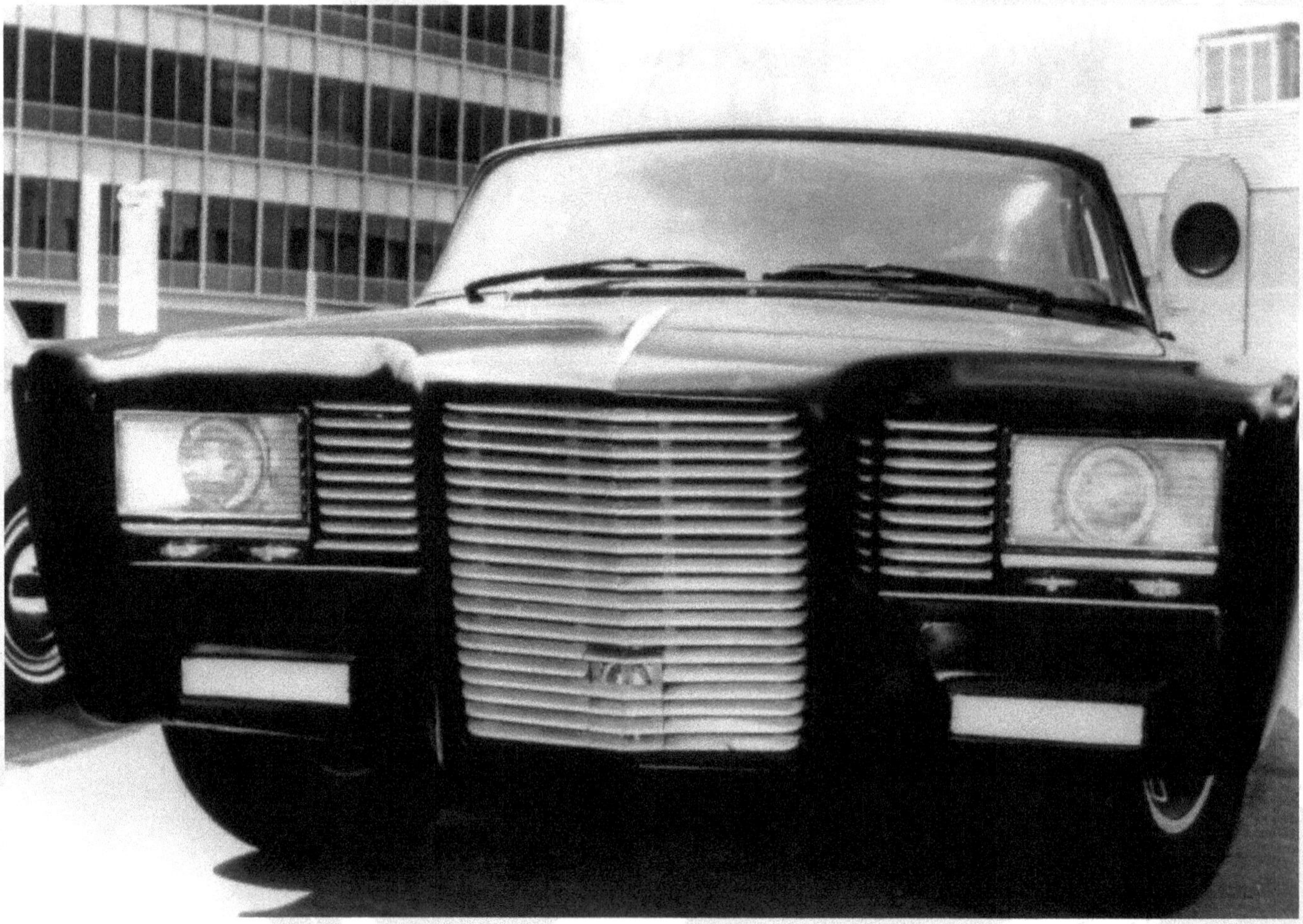

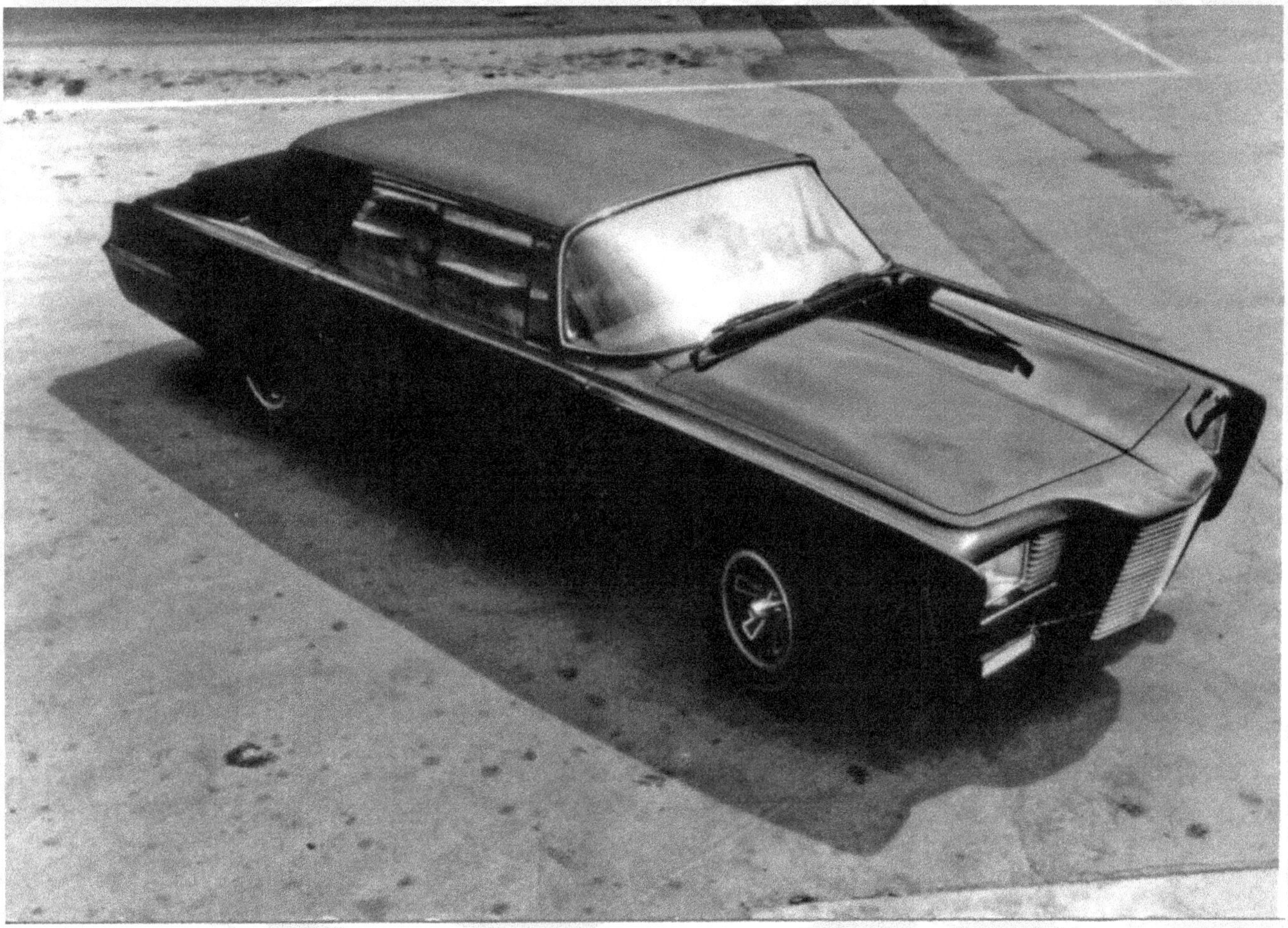

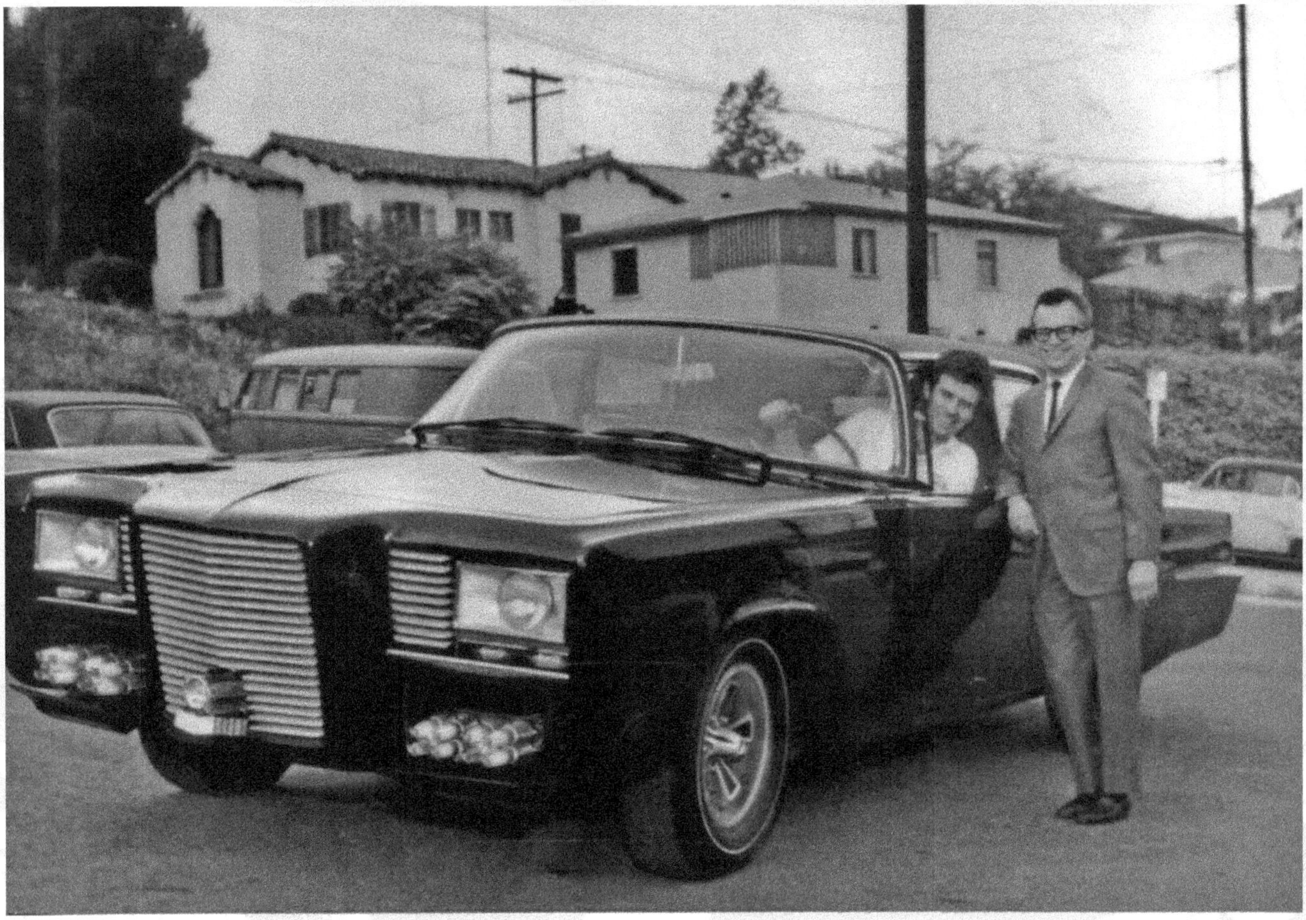

The Green Hornet Autograph Collection

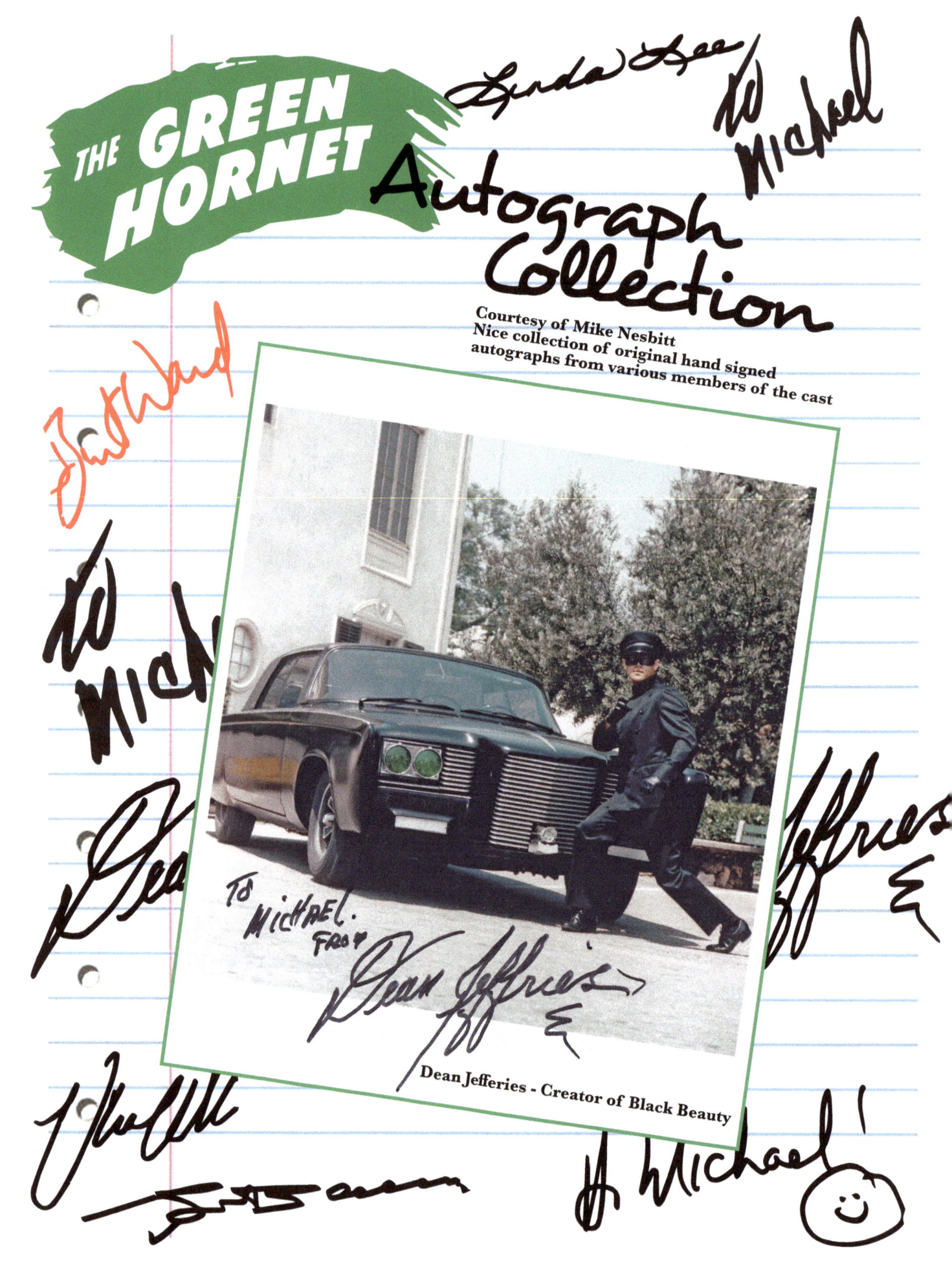

Courtesy of Mike Nesbitt
Nice collection of original hand signed autographs from various members of the cast

Dean Jefferies - Creator of Black Beauty

Allen Joe and Bruce Lee - Behind the scenes

Van Williams and Bruce Lee

Van Williams and Bruce Lee

Van Williams and Bruce Lee

Van Williams and Bruce Lee

Van Williams and Bruce Lee

Van Williams, Dean Jefferies and Bruce Lee

Gene Lebell and Bruce Lee

George Lee, Bruce Lee, Allen Joe and James Lee

ROBIN VS KATO
Behind the Scenes of the Battle of the Sidekicks!

By Jason McNeil

Hollywood legend has it that, in 1967, during the filming of Batman (Season 2, Episodes 51 and 52), which guest-starred Van Williams and Bruce Lee as The Green Hornet and Kato – a crossover that ABC hoped would draw Bat-fans to its NEW show about a costumed, crime-fighting duo – Bruce got very upset about the prospect of Kato losing a fight with Robin, and set about letting everyone know that he was going whip the Boy Wonder's spandex-clad ass for real!

The Tinseltown Rumor Mill being what it is, there are various versions of the story floating around, to the point where it has taken on the air of urban legend. So, we thought, why not hear it straight from the horse's mouth? Or, mouths, I suppose, would be more appropriate. Not one mouth, but two.

Since interviewing Bruce Lee is impossible for anyone besides, perhaps, "1986 Tawny Kitaen with a Ouija Board" and, sadly, Miss Kitaen, herself, having passed away last year (and Ami Dolenz won't return our calls....), we're left to draw from the first-hand accounts of two other men who were right there in the thick of it: Burt Ward (who, of course, played Robin the Boy Wonder) and Van Williams (who was Brit Reid/The Green Hornet.)

For our purposes, here, we enter into evidence two somewhat different remembrances of the day and events in question. Burt Ward's account is quoted from several sources, including his 1995 memoir, Boy Wonder: My Life in Tights, in which he takes time between bragging about his huge penis and claiming to be able to read 30,000 words a minute to regale the reader with the tale of Robin and Kato. As Van Williams has also crossed over to join Ms. Kitaen in the Choir Invisible, his remembrances are taken, verbatim, from several interviews where he discussed the day and events in question.

Give it a read, and you can make up your own mind.

Burt Ward: "Very few people know this bit of film fighting trivia, but Bruce Lee's first filmed fight was with me! The show was Batman and I, of course, was portraying Robin. Bruce was playing the Green Hornet's right-hand man, Kato, in the Batman two-parter, A Piece of the Action

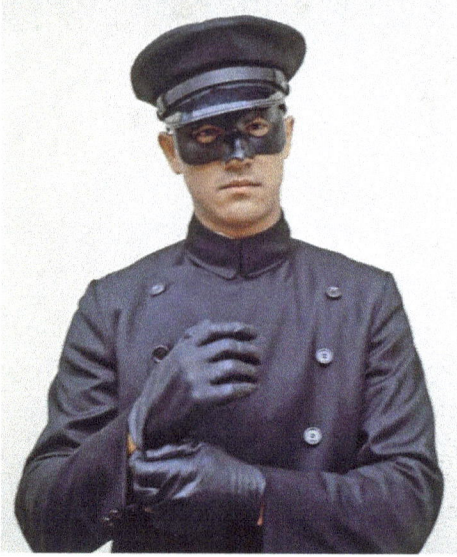

and Batman's Satisfaction."

Van Williams: "I was sitting and waiting for the gaffers to get the lighting done, and going into do a shot – Bruce wasn't in the shot, he was in his dressing room – a guy walks in, a messenger walks in, and he says 'Here.' I said 'What's that?' and he said 'Its the script.' I figured it was the script for the next show, so I threw it in the chair next to me, waited around, went in, did my thing, came back and sat down."

Burt Ward: "In a couple of inane news stories, I was portrayed as being in mortal fear of having to fight Bruce; they said he toyed with me as a cat might with a mouse. These journalistic incompetents failed to research their stories. Had they done so, they would have found that I had studied Kenpo karate from the age of fifteen and had received my brown belt before I ever tried out for the part of Robin."

Van Williams: "About the time I sat down, I heard this 'YARRRRRRHHH!' SCREAM! BANG! WHAM! You know, this that and the other, and you could hear the progression of him – Bruce, I found out later – leaving the sound stage – the slamming of the car door, the starting of the car, the screeching of the tires exiting the lot. And I said to my stand-in, 'What in the hell was all that for?' And he said 'You see that package?' And I said 'Yeah.' He said 'That package is where you're going over and being guest stars on the Batman. And you get into a fight with them, and you both lose.' And I said 'You've got to be kidding!'

Burt Ward: "Even more importantly, Bruce and I were friends and neighbors long before we filmed that scene. I sparred and trained with him at his apartment a few floors below. Not only did we live in the same building, but we found time in our schedules to go out for dinner with our wives."

Van Williams: "Bruce could not stand Burt Ward. Burt Ward had let everybody know that he could wipe Kato's butt all over the lot. That he was this big karate expert and he knew a lot more about it than Bruce did. And those little things trickle back, and we hear them, and Bruce got more uptight about it."

Burt Ward: "Bruce liked to take us to Chinatown in downtown Los Angeles. He always ordered special things not on the menu for Caucasians, and he insisted on paying the bill."

Van Williams: "So, anyway, as you say, there was a Mexican standoff on it – Bruce wouldn't do it. He just flat refused to do it. And, you know, I kind of admired him to do it, because it was the most ridiculous thing in the world, because Robin didn't have any expertise at fighting or anything else that I knew of. And for this fighting machine to go over there and lose to him was a real put-down for Bruce. And I could see his position. So I sided with him. I said 'Hey, I'm with Bruce.'"

Burt Ward: "We also spent days comparing exercise and sparring techniques, and our fight scene on film was barely more than a toned-down version of the real sparring we did on the set."

Van Williams: "Bruce could be very intimidating, and he stormed into that set, he sat down and he stared at Burt and, I tell ya, I think Burt wet his pants! I really do, The word was out that he did. And Burt was so scared that he wouldn't work. They finally talked him out of it, that

'Mr. Lee was not going to hurt you and kick you in the face and in the balls and everything else, and, you know, he was not going to do that. We're going to film this and everybody's going to be happy.' But Bruce just intimidated the heck out of him, and I don't think he ever lived that down! Because everybody on the lot knew he was absolutely petrified of Bruce Lee."

About the author:
Jason McNeil is an actor, writer and martial artist who was just kidding about Ami Dolenz "not returning our calls." Ami Dolenz is a lovely and talented woman who, frankly, Jason was disinclined to call for something as silly as "Using the Ouija board skills she displayed in 1993"s Witchboard 2: The Devil's Doorway to contact Bruce Lee beyond the grave" because she's married to kickboxing champ Jerry Trimble, who is such a karate badass that he could, theoretically, storm onto set, sit down, stare at Jas and make him wet his pants. And we don't think Jas would ever live that down.

"LET'S GO, KATO!"
THE LONG, STRANGE TRIP OF THE GREEN HORNET'S SUPER-CAR!

By Jason McNeil

GREEN HORNET AND KATO AND THEIR FAMOUS CRIME FIGHTING CAR, DIRECT FROM HOLLYWOOD AND TV, THE WORLD FAMOUS DEBUT AT THE CHICAGO HISTORICAL ANTIQUE AUTOMOBILE VALLEY ROAD, HIGHLAND PARK, ILL. VAN WILLIAMS STAR "GREEN HORNET" AND BRUCE LEE AS HIS FAITHFUL SERVAN CURRENT STAR OF A HOST OF KUNG-FU TYPE MOVIES. TH A KIND CREATION, BUILT SPECIAL FOR THE T.V. SERIES BY G THE MUSEUM IS OPEN 7 DAYS A WEEK, 9 A.M. to 6 P.M.

Chicago Historical Antique
Automobile Museum Inc.
3160 Skokie Valley Road
Highland Park, Illinois 60035
Tel. (312) 433-4400

While Kato (played by Bruce Lee – but then you already knew that) served as an infinitely more ass-kicking version of Robin to the Green Hornet's Batman, he also literally "served" as both manservant and, oddly, chauffeur to both Britt Reid and his green masked and fedora-ed crime fighting alter-ego! (Its as if The Boy Wonder was both Dick Grayson and Alfred.)

Yes, I said chauffeur While billionaire Bruce Wayne tore up the streets of Gotham City behind the wheel of the Batmobile, the Green Hornet did what "proper" rich guys do and had his "Kung-Fu Man Friday" drive him from crime scene to crime scene to, inevitably, the "villain of the week's" secret lair, watching the streets roll by while contemplating whatever it is that rich guys think about from the back seats of fancy cars. Probably something to do with inheritance taxes.

Be that as it may, the Green Hornet's crime-fighting super-car, bearing the elegant name "The Black Beauty," was an awesome vehicle in its own right, featuring built-in crime fighting gear, from green beamed headlights to rocket launchers, all built into a sleek, sexy black 1966 Chrysler Imperial hardtop that made the Batmobile, by comparison, look at bit like a rodeo clown at a black tie dinner. And, when counting the automotive cool points, need we remind you DRIVEN BY BRUCE EFFIN LEE?

For all its awesome power and sleek sexiness, though, the Black Beauty rose fast and fell hard, becoming something of an automotive Leif Garrett. When The Green Hornet was canceled after only one season, the Black Beauty literally hit the Hollywood skids, moving from garage to garage, from driveway to junk yard to another junk yard, to yet another junkyard, before finally being rediscovered, restored to its former glory and put on a proper pedestal for superhero fans and automotive enthusiasts alike to appreciate.

But, first things first. Allow us at Eastern Heroes to properly introduce you to The Black Beauty, then we can get to all the "third act of Behind the Music" sordidness, and our Hero Car's eventual redemption.

RISE

Although it appeared in both the original Green Hornet radio series and movie serials (where it was mostly just "fast" and capable of outrunning police cars), the Black Beauty really came into its own when ABC decided to capitalize on the massive popularity of their 1966 Batman series by... well, basically trying to do a different version of the same show. In addition to a mask wearing crime fighter and his faithful sidekick, the Green Hornet ALSO had his own crime-fighting car, so the network went all in and hired Dean Jeffries to make Britt Reid his very own version of the Batmobile! In fact the network went so "all in" that they reportedly paid Jeffries $50,000 US (that's nearly half a million in today's dollars!), to outfit the new crime fighting super-car with not only the aforementioned green headlights and rockets, but also add on enough other good guy gadgetry to make Q blush – knockout gas nozzles, explosive rockets, a flying remote surveillance disc thingy it could launch whenever the plot needed to be sped up a little, and on and on and on! In addition, the car's paint job consisted of – no kidding – 30 COATS of "metal flake pure black green pearl of essence lacquer hand-rubbed to a high gloss."

In the show, the Black Beauty was stored on a weird, upside-down trap door thingy under Britt Reid's garage. When he flipped a switch, the floor of the garage would literally flip over, replacing Britt's "civilian" car with the Black Beauty, which Kato would then drive thru a hidden rear door and "enter the street from behind a billboard advertising the fictitious product Kissin' Candy Mints – with the slogan 'How sweet they are' - that was cleverly designed to separate down the middle and rejoin." Then Kato would drive his boss to wherever they had to go that week to fight crime. (And Kato would also do most of the fighting. But, let us not digress....)

CRASH!

After only one season, however, The Green Hornet was canceled and the Black Beauty suddenly found itself jobless, drifting aimlessly around Hollywood, like so many "here today, gone tomorrows" before it, moving from garage to garage like a four-wheeled Corey Haim.

As the years and decades passed, even though the Black Beauty remained in excellent shape mechanically, having logged only 17,000 miles (approximately 27,350 km) and still having its original custom wheels and most of the custom body mods Jeffries had done for the show, the body became "badly weathered" and "was something of an eyesore for many years." (Which again begs the Leif Garrett comparison... but let's not get sidetracked.) Even its status as a "classic car" didn't stop it from going "from junkyard to junkyard" and, before that, it had moved from the FOX lot to "a woman's parking lot" where it was kept "with little or no maintenance."

In the early 90s, Inside Kung-Fu magazine's Editor-in-Chief, Dave Cater, was contacted by the then-current owner of the Black Beauty, asking if he and/or the magazine would be interested in buying it. "The guy lived in Santa Clarita," recalls Cater, "and kept it in his garage." Cater contacted Van Williams (who played the Green Hornet in the series - but you know that) and asked if he would be interested in buying it, but "Van said he didn't need it" says Cater. "At the time, he was struggling with some health issues, and he moved shortly thereafter."

Perhaps the most obvious question, of course, is did anyone make the same offer to Bruce Lee's widow, Linda, or his children, Brandon and Shannon. Not to his knowledge, says Cater. "The Lee's were just getting into the game, then. Very much on the outside."

RESURRECTION

In 1992, a Green Hornet uber-fan named Dan Goodman bought the Black Beauty from the "former transportation director of Twentieth Century Fox" for the princely sum of $10,000 and took the decrepit super-car back to the guy who gave it the original 30 coats of paint, Dan Jeffries!

Jeffries set about restoring the Black Beauty to its original glory (well, more or less – a few of the gadgets don't work anymore, but why split hairs?) and they all lived happily ever after. Right? Well, not exactly.

For reasons that differ wildly, depending on whose attorney you're speaking to, Goodman and Jeffries spent much of the next 20 years suing each other, enmeshing the Green Hornet-mobile in a decades long tangle of litigation and counter-litigation, using terms like "cost overruns" and "rights to the Black Beauty name and likeness." Frankly, its all

boring lawyer shit that we won't bore you with.

Suffice it to say that the light at the end of the legal tunnel finally shone through, and the Black Beauty, restored to its shining state of mid-60s glory, has been placed upon a well-deserved pedestal, before which all may kneel and pay homage.

Or, y'know... at least snap a selfie.

The Black Beauty currently resides at the Petersen Automotive Museum in Los Angeles, California, alongside the Batmobile and a myriad of its Hollywood automotive brethren. If you're ever in Tinseltown, do yourself a favor and check out the Petersen Museum – you'll be glad you did. Go ahead, snap a selfie. Snap two.

Then stand back and marvel at the magnificence that is the Black Beauty and think: "DAMMMMMMNNNN! Bruce Lee used to drive that thing!

The Petersen Automotive Museum is located at 6060 Wilshire Blvd, Los Angeles, California 90036. For more information, go online to www.petersen.org

About the author
Jason McNeil is an actor, writer and martial artist who – no shit! - once took a business call as a "Superman Expert."

THE GREEN HORNET SCREEN TEST

By Simon Pritchard

Bruce Lee's screen test for Green Hornet is infamous. It created interest in Hollywood four years prior to Bruce filming The Big Boss with Golden Harvest in Hong Kong. The original screen test for the Green Hornet was meant to be two scenes, an interview and a demonstration. The screen

test ended up as three scenes as, the second scene, they could not get the camera angles right when demonstrating with a member of the production. The third scene was Bruce demonstrating alone.

The screen test is approximately a little over eight minutes dependent on the YouTube video you watch. Within this time, Bruce explains his philosophy, shows his fighting skills and two traditional animal forms making it one of the best screen tests ever.

Scene I – The interview
Interviewer: "Now Bruce, Just look right into the camera lens right here, and tell us your name, your age, and where you were born."

Bruce: "My last name is Lee, Bruce Lee. I was born in San Francisco in 1940. I am 24 right now."

It is widely accepted that this screen test was filmed in 1964. I believe that this was recorded between 1st February 1965 and 1st May 1965 due the time line and conversation below:
Interviewer: "Now look at me Bruce as we talk. I understand you've just had a baby boy?"

Bruce: "Yeah"

Interviewer: "And you've lost a little sleep over it or what have you?"

Bruce: "Every night!"

• 27th November 1940 – Bruce was born.
• 1st January 1959 to 26th November 1959 – Bruce went to America at 18 years of age.
• 27th November 1964 – Bruce would have been 24 years of age.
• 1st February 1965 – Brandon Bruce Lee was born. Brandon would have on average slept through the night after three months*.

Eluding that the interview must be have between 1st February 1965 and 1st May 1965.
• 27th November 1965 – Bruce would have been 25 years of age.
• 9th September 1966 to 24th March 1967 – The first episode of Green Hornet, "The Silent Gun", premiered on American TV, until the last episode "The Hornet and the Firefly". 26 episodes were made in total.

*Information obtained from www.standford-childrens.org
Bruce mentions that due to all the noise in Hong Kong the best time for filming was 12am to 5am. They move on to talking about kung fu and the differences to Japanese styles.

Interviewer: "Now you told me earlier today that karate and ju-jitsu are not the most powerful or best forms of oriental fighting. What is the most powerful or best form?"

Bruce: "Well, it's bad to say the 'best' but in my opinion kung fu is pretty good!"

Interviewer: "Can you tell us a little bit about kung fu?"

Bruce: "Well, kung fu is originated in China. It is the ancestor of karate and ju-jitsu. It's more of a complete system and it's more fluid. By that I mean there's more flowing; there is continuity in movement instead of one movement, two movement and so on".

Interviewer: "Would you look right into the camera lens and explain the principle of the glass of water as it applies in kung fu?"

Bruce: "Well kung fu, the best example will be a glass of water. Why? Because water is the softest substance in the world, but yet can penetrate the hardest rock or anything! Granite, you name it. Water also is insubstantial; by that I mean you cannot grasp hold of it. You cannot punch it and hurt it. So every kung fu man is trying to do that. To be soft like water and flexible and adapt himself to the opponent".

Camera reel ends.

Scene II – The demonstration part one

The interviewer first asks about traditional Chinese theatre and Bruce explains how the movements and the demeanor of the characters tell the audience which characters are which. Bruce demonstrates the difference between the movements of a warrior and a scholar.

They move on to kung fu and a member of the production enters for Bruce to demonstrate on. The guy looks like the typical old conservative 1960's dude with Buddy Holly thick black-rimmed glasses. In fairness, the guy hardly flinches! Whilst Bruce is demonstrating the Director is moving them around the stage for the right camera angle but it was not working so Bruce did it solo in Scene III.

Bruce: "They're various types of strikes dependent on where you strike, depends on what weapon you will be using"

- "To the eyes, you'll use fingers"
- "Or straight to the face from the waist everything on"
- "And then, there is an arm strike, using the waist again, into a backfist"
- "And then of course kung fu is very sneaky. You know the Chinese; they all hit low from high, hit to the groin!"

Bruce then demonstrates all four moves in one motion.

Bruce: "Then of course they use legs. Straight at the groin or come up, or if I can stand back a little bit; they STOMP it on you and come back.

Camera reel ends.

Scene III – The demonstration part two

Scene starts with Bruce explaining why he prefers kung fu over karate and ju-jitsu. Bruce explains that due to the fast, minimal movement and simplicity of kung fu, is superior over the many steps of karate and ju-jitsu.

Interviewer: "Now can you show me once again some more movements?"

Bruce: "Well kung fu can be practiced alone or with a partner. Practicing alone involves forms. Some imitate crane, a monkey, a praying mantis"

Bruce then demonstrates a part of Crane form.

Bruce ends with a part of the Tiger form.

Camera reel ends.

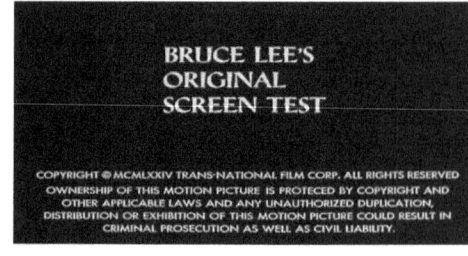

The *Great* Green Hornet find!
Hector Martinez

Hector Martinez struck out gold when he managed to purchase this rare photo directly from a lady on "Etsy" who told him that she acquired this photo from the estate of the gentleman in the photo holding the clapperboard next to Bruce Lee. Hector goes on to explain...

In the photo is the always dapper and strikingly handsome Bruce Lee standing next to the second assistant camera man aka the "clapper loader" holding the clapperboard with the date of August 22, 1966 (exactly one month before the series premiered on abc.) The first episode of the Green Hornet titled "The Silent Gun" premiered on September 9th so we are more than sure that this photo was taken during Bruce's very charismatic and enthusiastic invitation to the viewer's when he says "Join me on most of these abc stations." Now the hot topic on social media is the mystery behind the "Mercy Crusade" and what does it have to do with Bruce Lee and The Green Hornet? So I did a bit of research and found that the promo spot was to air during Chicago's 1966 "Charity Crusade" which was a charity event aimed at raising funds for the Jewish community. At this time Bruce was on a promotional tour along with Van Williams taking part in the crusade's parade. It's such a fine photo and a strong reminder that the quest for Bruce Lee information continues with much left to be learned about this fascinating human being!

The Green Hornet

John Negron's Memorabilia Section

It gives me great pleasure to present one of the finest collections of Green Hornet memorabilia I have ever seen. The collection belongs to my good friend John Negron, who took the time out to photograph this part of his Bruce lee collection.

The collection spanning over many years of collecting will allow others to see the vast amount of merchandise that has been available pertaining to the TV show "The Green Hornet".

I hope you enjoy looking at the many items as much as I did putting this section together

Rick Baker

BLACK BEAUTY CAR

BOARD GAMES AND ENTERTAINMENT

DISPLAY CABINETS

DISPLAY CABINETS

DISPLAY CABINETS

DISPLAY CABINETS

DISPLAY CABINETS

FIGURES

JOHN WITH HIS COLLECTION

MAGAZINES & COMICS

MAGAZINES & COMICS

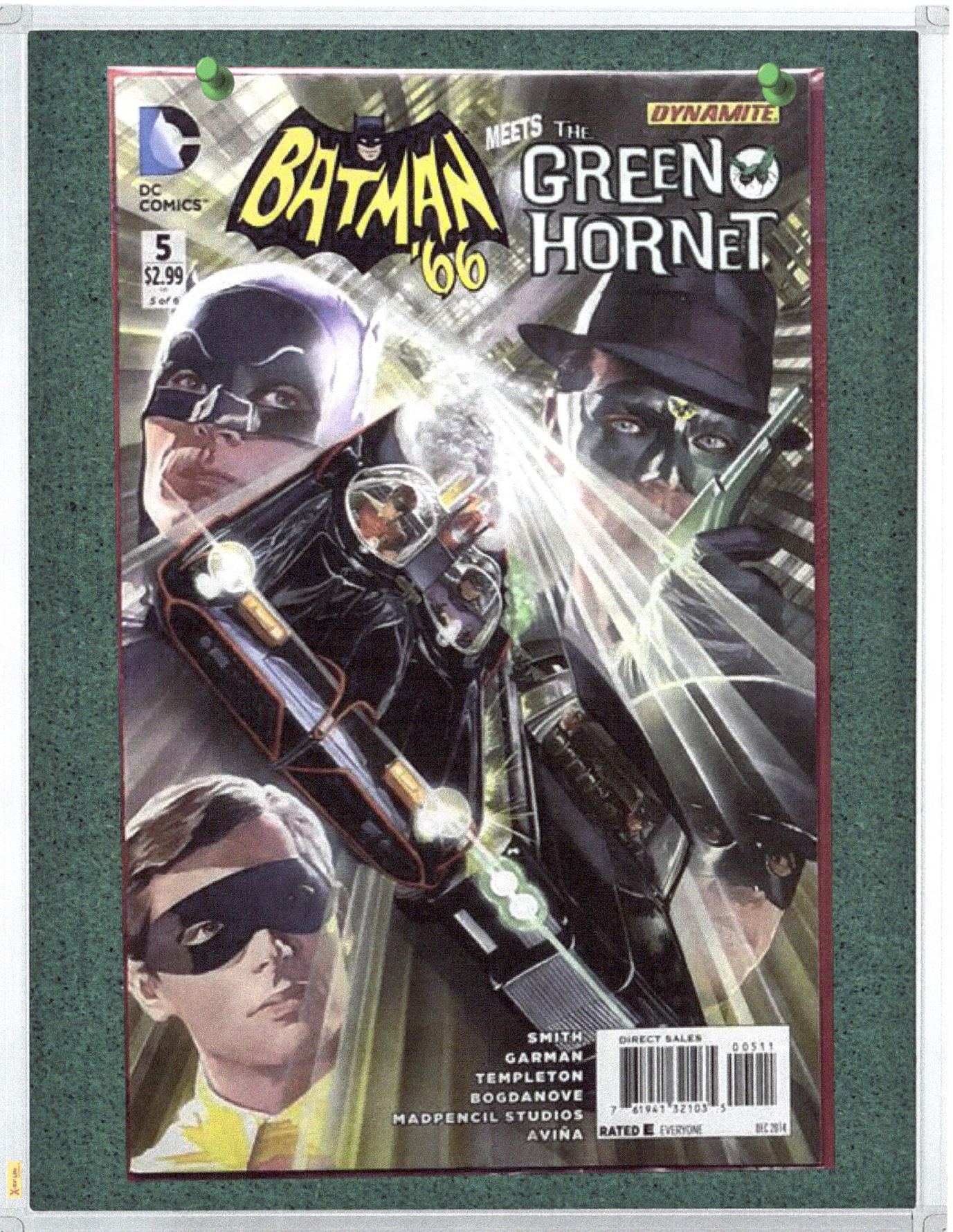

MAGAZINES & COMICS

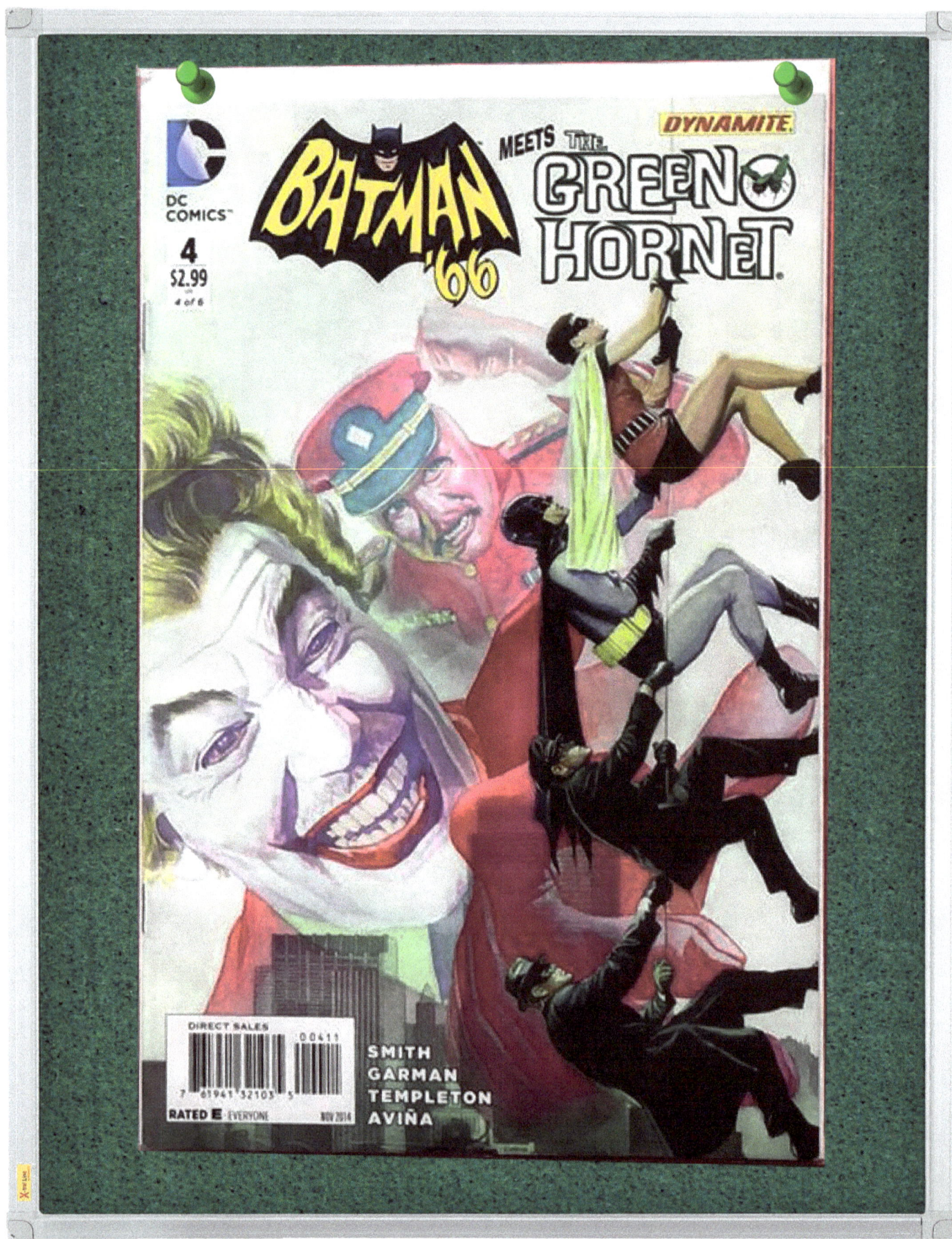

MAGAZINES & COMICS

MAGAZINES & COMICS

MAGAZINES & COMICS

MAGAZINES & COMICS

MISCELLANEOUS

MISCELLANEOUS

MISCELLANEOUS

MISCELLANEOUS

MISCELLANEOUS

PHOTOGRAPHS

RECORDS, SIGNED PHOTOS & T-SHIRTS

THE GERMAN COLLECTOR

Thomas Gross

Once again! For this "Green Hornet" special. Thomas Gross has also been kind enough to share some of his Green Hornet memorabilia consisting of Lobby Cards and posters from around the world.

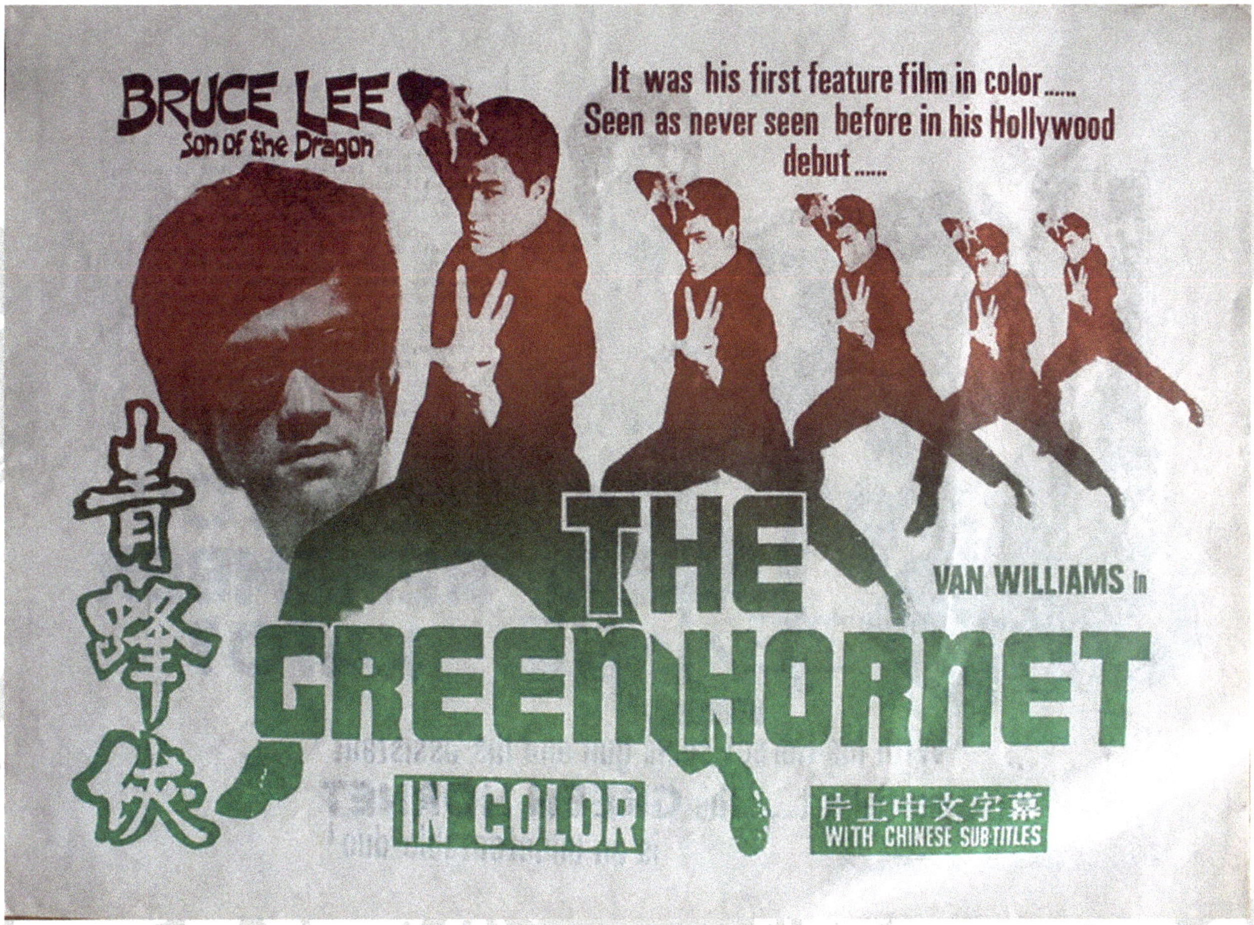
BRUCE LEE
Son of the Dragon
It was his first feature film in color......
Seen as never seen before in his Hollywood debut......
青蜂俠
THE GREEN HORNET
VAN WILLIAMS in
IN COLOR
片上中文字幕
WITH CHINESE SUB-TITLES

--- The Story---
The T.V. series "The Green Hornet" starring Van Williams and Bruce Lee as Kato was very successful way back many years ago.
In this color full-length feature,the audiences will once again see the young Bruce Lee,handsome and completely unspoilt.
"THE GREEN HORNET" is known and feared in the underworld of America.He,and his assistant,Kato(Bruce Lee) pledge to eliminate the gangs,the drug pushers and the secert societies,known in Chinatown as the Tongs.
The film has three sequences in which Bruce Lee appears.In each,he demonstrates effectively the various martial arts.In the final sequence,his fight to a finish with the leader of the tongs,showed on the screen for the first time,what karate and kungfu were all about.
To all fans of Bruce Lee and Green Hornet, this is a 'must' movie brought back specially for you
DO YOU REMEMBER KATO?
李小龍
領銜主演
With his Hornet sonic gun and his assistant martial art....... the GREEN HORNET is an undefeatable duo!
Printed by Lian Pong Printing & Co.
TO-NIGHT AT 7.15

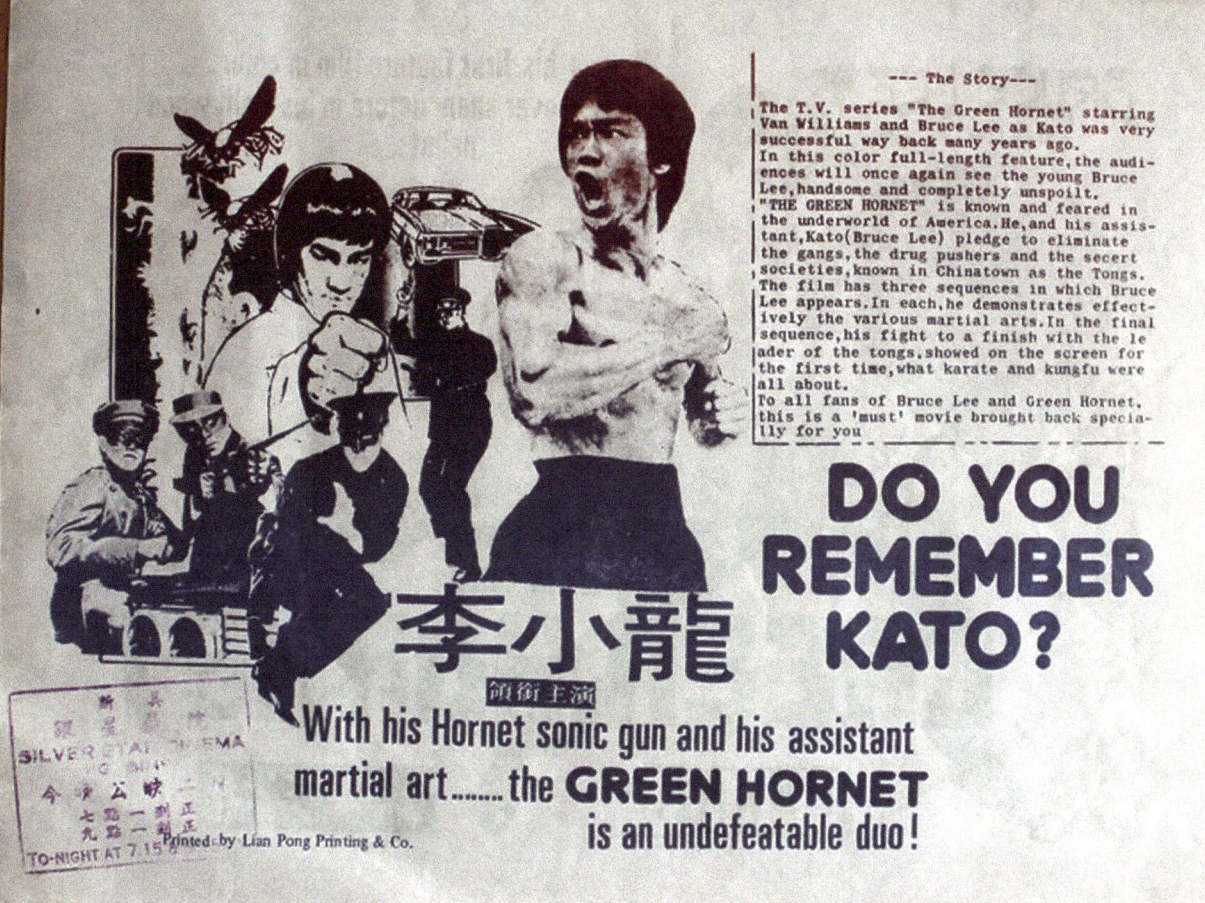

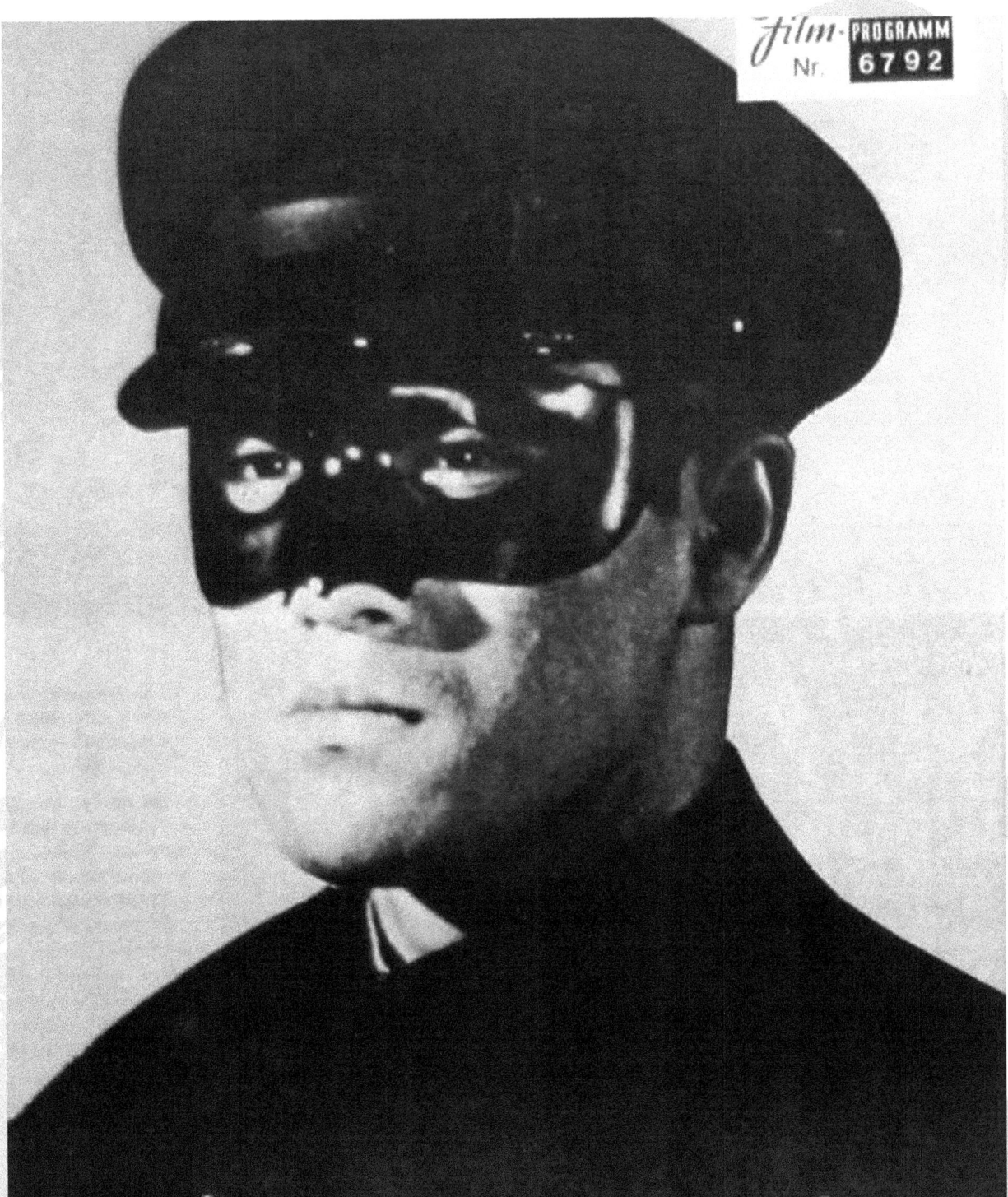

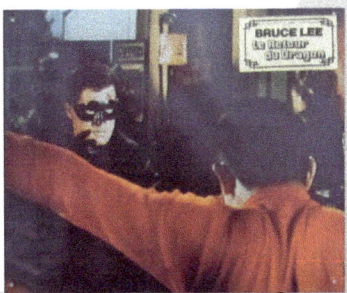

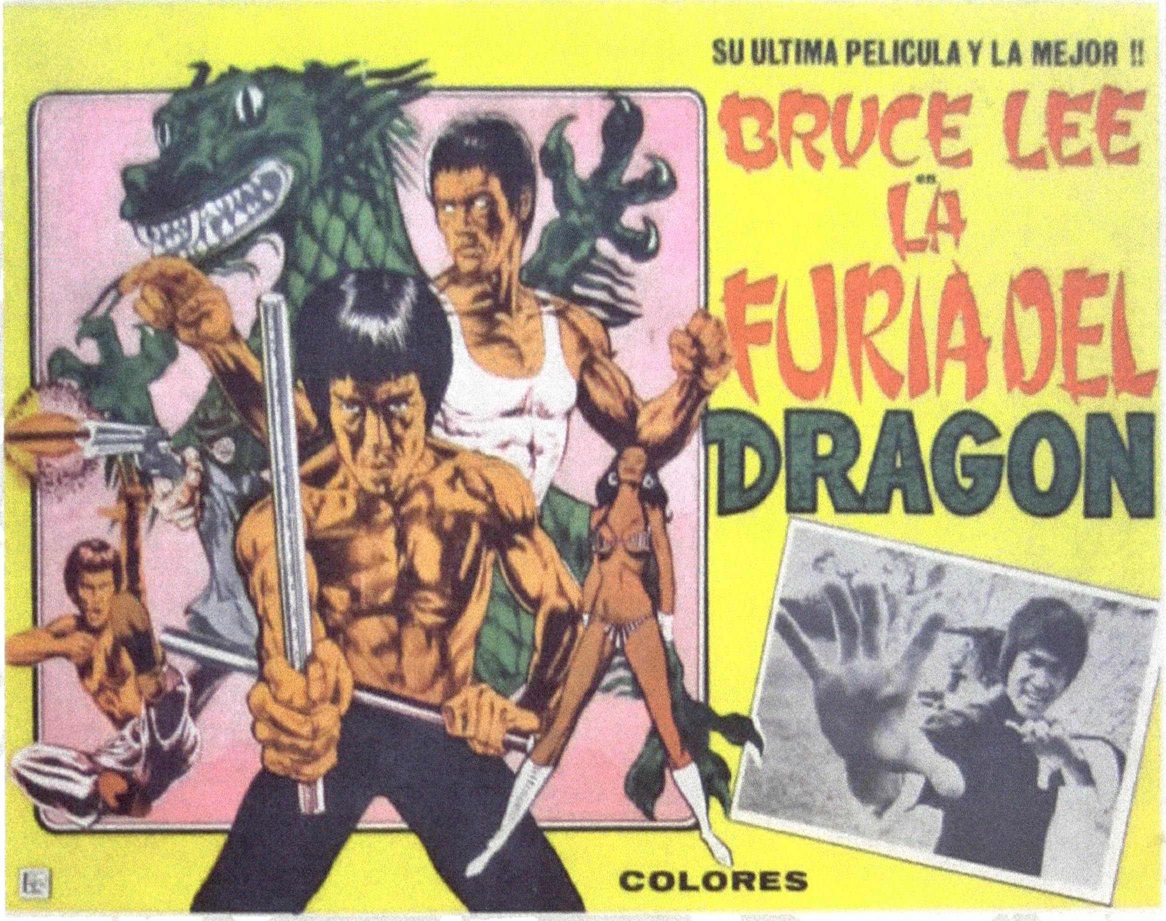

With his Hornet sonic gun and h

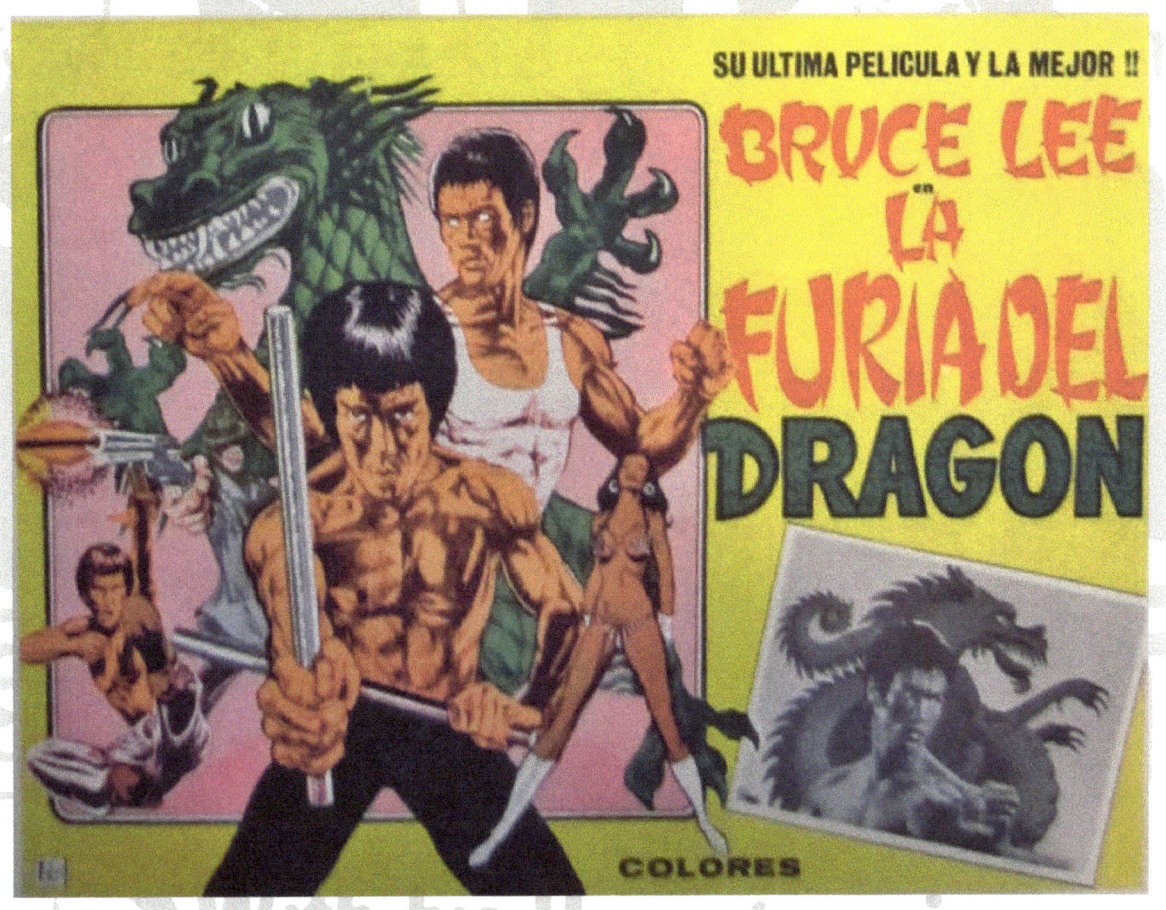

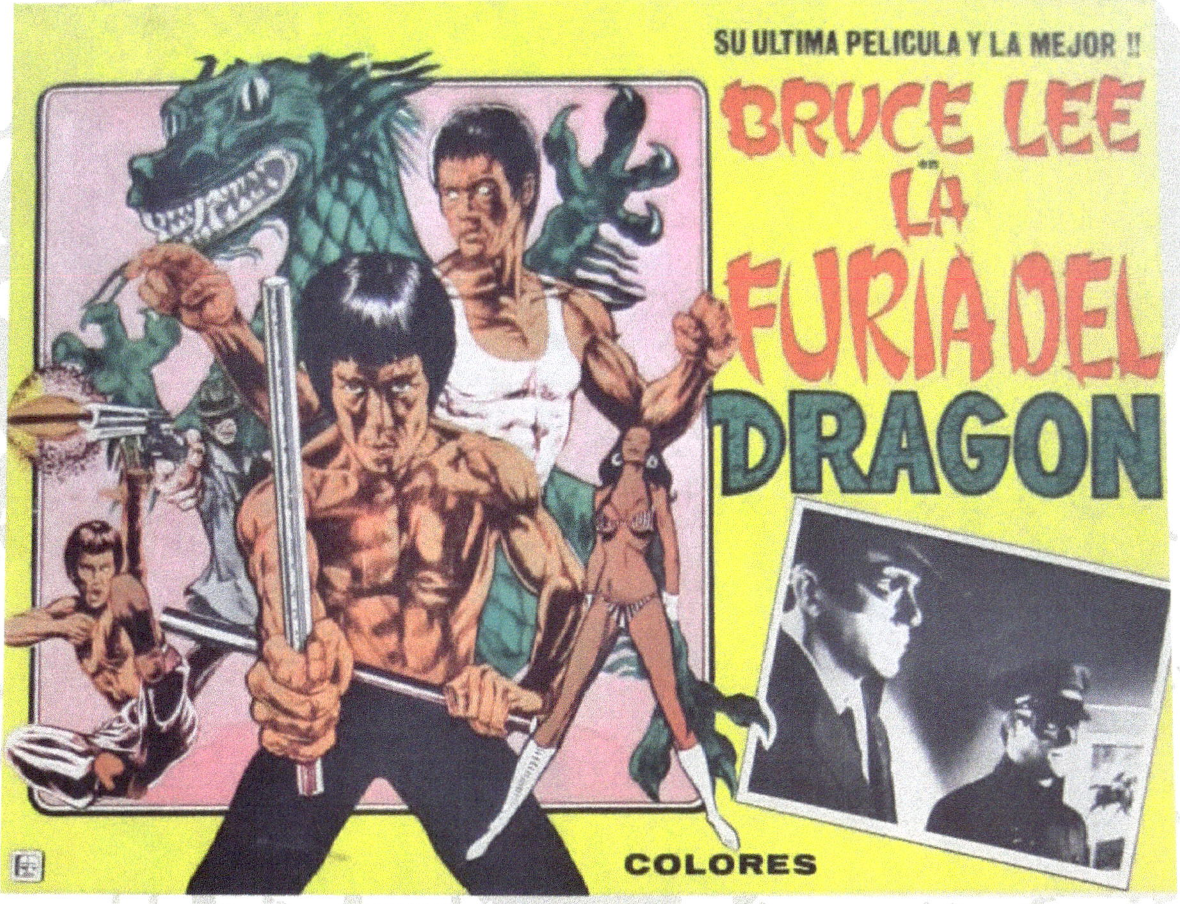
SU ULTIMA PELICULA Y LA MEJOR !!
BRUCE LEE
en
LA
FURIA DEL
DRAGON
COLORES

SU ULTIMA PELICULA Y LA MEJOR !!
BRUCE LEE
en
LA
FURIA DEL
DRAGON
COLORES

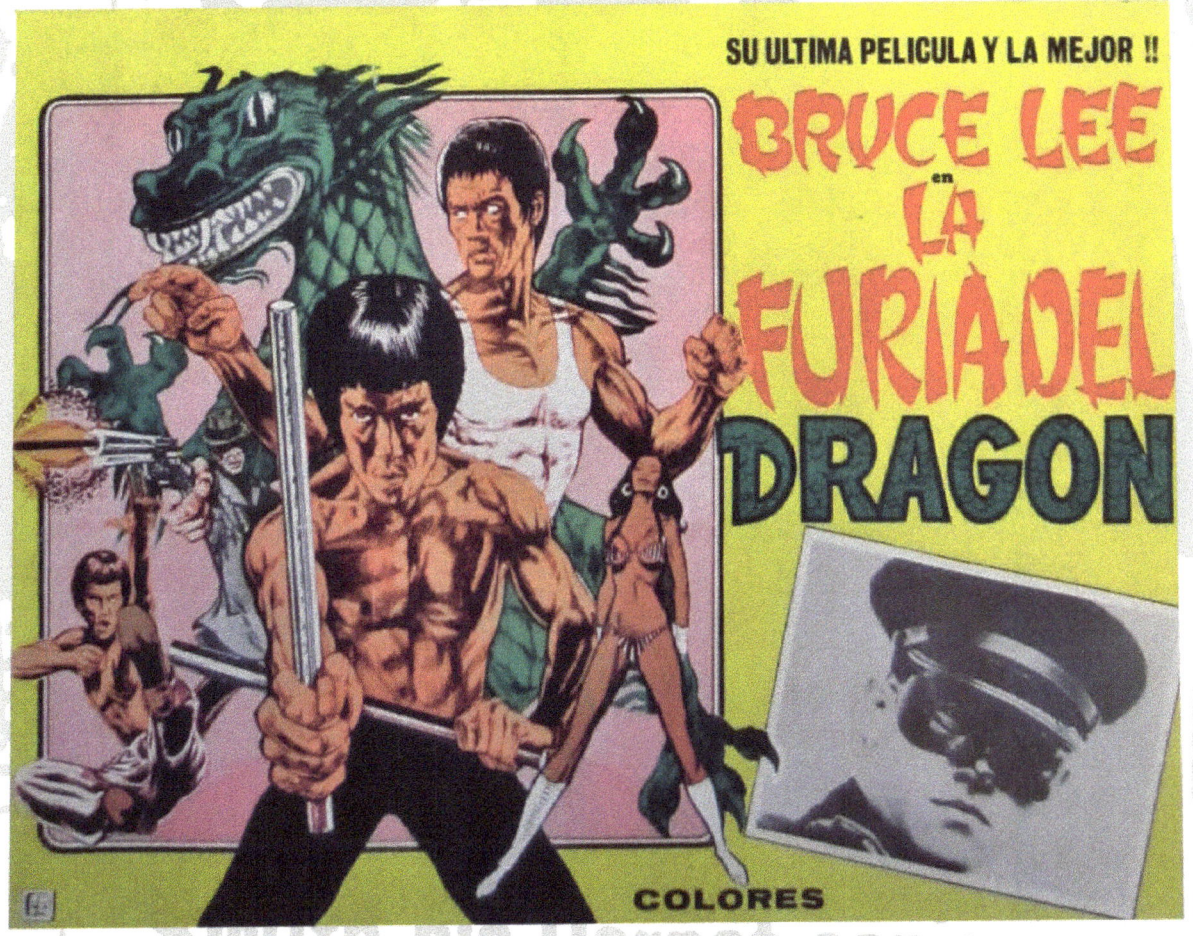

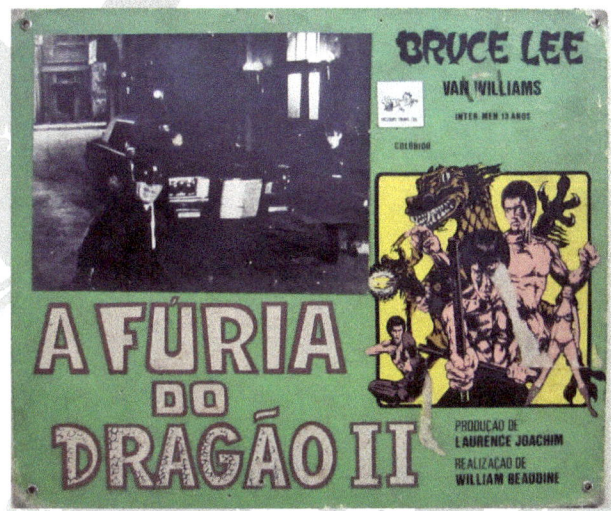

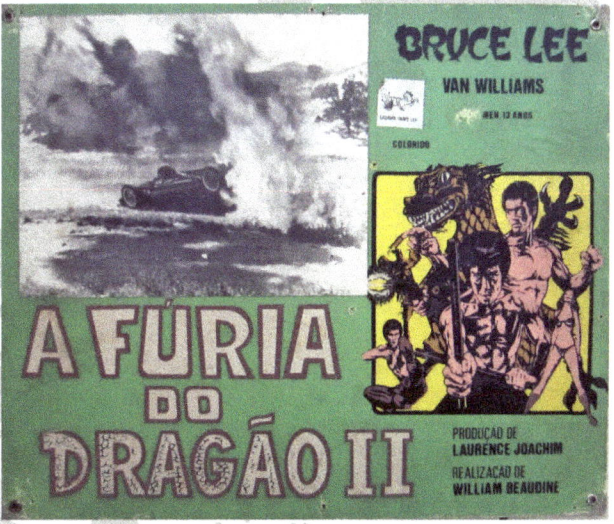

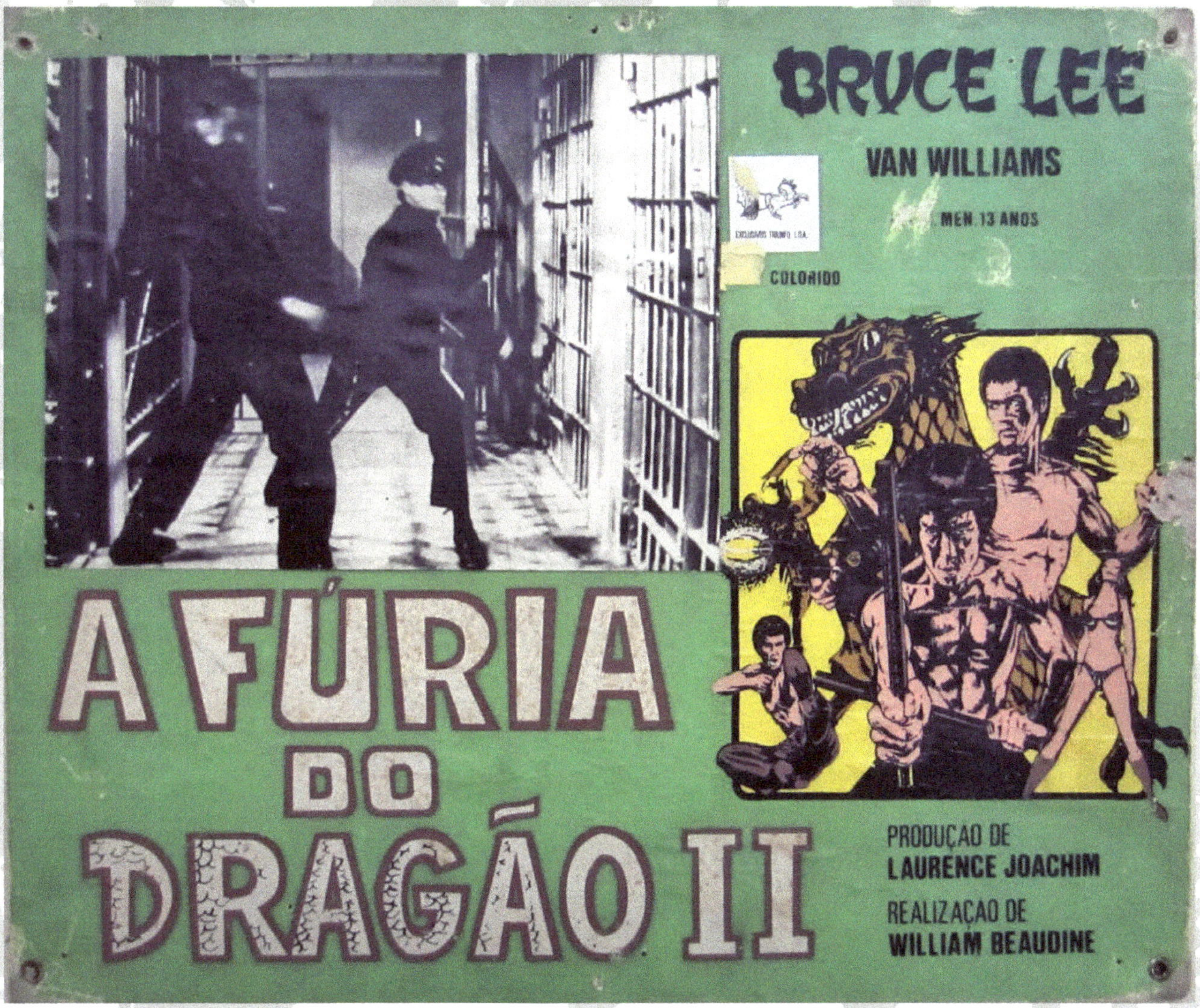

With his Hornet sonic gun and h

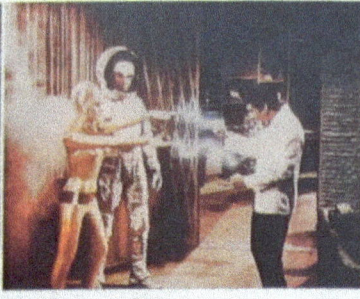

Američki film u boji

OSVETA ZELENOG OBADA
(FURY OF THE DRAGON)

Režiser WILLIAM BEAUDINE

Rod PARODIJA AKCIONOG FILMA

Trajanje 85 minuta

U glavnim ulogama: BRUCE LEE i VAN WILLIAMS

Film je rađen prema televizijskoj seriji koja je imala velik uspjeh u SAD. Jedan dio serije obuhvaćen je filmom »KUNG FU – ZELENI OBAD«. »OSVETA ZELENOG OBADA« je nastavak avantura maskiranog izdavača (Van Williams) i njegovog šofera Katoa (Bruce Lee) koji vode dvostruki život.

BRUCE LEE u filmu
KUNG FU ZELENI OBAD

Američki film u koloru

KUNG FU – ZELENI OBAD
(THE GREEN HORNET)

Trajanje: 85 minuta

Glazba: AL HIRT
Režiser: NORMAN FOSTER

U glavnim ulogama:
BRUCE LEE
VAN WILLIAMS

Sadržaj:

Visoki, naočiti izdavač (Van Williams) i njegov kineski posvojni sinak i šofer Kato (Bruce Lee) vode dvostruki život: za javnost oni su mirni i poslovni ljudi, a u stvarnosti oni su neumoljivi izvršioci pravde tamo gdje policija nije u stanju presjeći mreže zločina. Oni djeluju pod maskama sa zaštitnim znakom zelenog obada i u nizu uzbudljivih sudara savladavaju daleko premoćnije protivnike iz redova gangsterskog podzemlja, fantastičnih znanstvenika koji se žele dokopati H-bombe i orjentalnih majstora karate i kung-fu vještina.

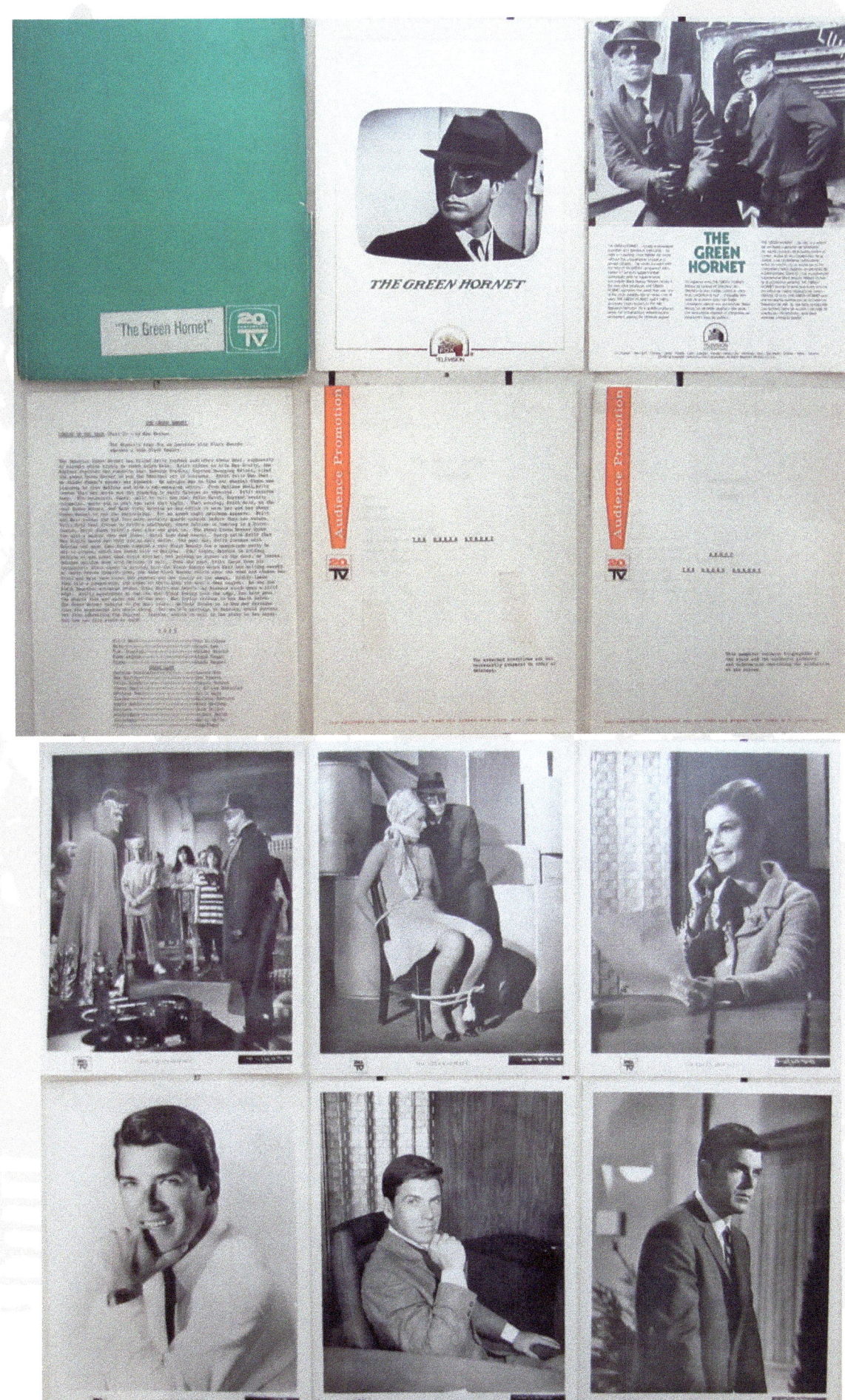

The Fanatical Dragon Presents..
Five Fingers of Discs Meets the Green Hornet

"He hunts the biggest of all game: public enemies who try to destroy our America... With his faithful valet Kato, Britt Reid, daring young publisher, matches wits with the Underworld, risking his life so that criminals and racketeers within the law may feel its weight by the sting of the Green Hornet!... Ride with Britt Reid as he races toward another thrilling adventure! The Green Hornet strikes again!"

For reasons seemingly only known to TV executives, Movie Studios and psychics, the original 26 Episode single season of The Green Hornet TV show starring Bruce Lee which has inspired this very Special Issue you hold in your hands now, has never in the many years since it's original airing and the subsequent rise of home entertainment and digital media, had a complete, official DVD or Blu-ray release in any territory. Now given how many different incarnations of Bruce's HK movies we've seen over the years, across all formats, it's a safe bet that a solid market does exist for such a release, but as of the date of writing this article, there is nothing on the horizon to suggest we'll see one anytime soon.

So what then can the ardent Bruce Lee Green Hornet fans amongst us do to satiate our collecting cravings??
Fear not Dear Friends, there are still a fair few bits and pieces of Bruce related Green Hornet video and memorabilia out there, all relatively readily available to scratch that Kato itch…
I've rounded up a few of the most notable examples, there are many, many more, but these are the ones that mostly won't break the bank, and can all be found pretty easily..

1) Batman The Complete TV Series Boxset

This was the other Classic and arguably more famous William Dozier produced TV show that languished in the vaults of Fox studios for decades before the rights battles could be sorted out and it could finally be given a worthy release. It represents not only the single best hope we have of a similar, smaller Green Hornet Boxset appearing sometime in the future, but it also contains the best quality example available of a few of the Green Hornet episodes inside it. Well almost, if we're splitting hairs, it's actually The Batman episodes of the two produced crossover specials made between the two shows.

The 120 episodes contained here never looked or sounded better and it's now a pretty reasonably priced boxset given it's been out for a while and is still readily available in the UK and US.
It is currently your only option to see a (fleeting) glimpse of Bruce's Kato on Blu-ray so far…

The boxset has 3 hours worth of bonus material, a mixture of interviews with the Cast and Crew, with extensive time given over to leading man Adam West along with features dedicated to the vast array of memorabilia produced for the show along with contributions from various celebrities who all recall their favourite memories of the series.
I'm pretty confident in guessing that if you're a fan of the original Green Hornet show, chances are you'll also be a fan of the 60's Batman series. Adam West and Burt Ward revelled in the super camp and very tongue in cheek nature of the show and it's still a delight to watch today. I'm sure just as I did, many of you grew up enjoying reruns of the show on TV, and it actually still

holds up far more respectably than the 90's Batman movies which when viewed now are actually every bit as camp as the TV series which proceeded them.

The member berries are strong indeed with this one.

2) The Green Hornet TV Show 'movie' DVDs

There are two old (and of somewhat questionable authenticity) compilation DVD's that rather crudely snip together all the Bruce Lee Moments from the Green Hornet show into two 90 min chunks. These are usually misleadingly labelled as 'movies' they are not. They certainly do have lots of great clips of Bruce from the show, but edited in such a way as to make next to no sense when viewed as a whole. And the quality, even for DVD, is poor. The big saving grace is these are incredibly cheap, usually £3-£5. One disc is simply called 'The Green Hornet', the other 'The Fury of The Dragon'. I'm including these two purely for the sake of being as thorough as I can, I'm loathe to recommend them, they're pretty shoddily put together and the show frankly deserves so, so much better. File these two under the category of Brucesploitation rather than traditional releases.

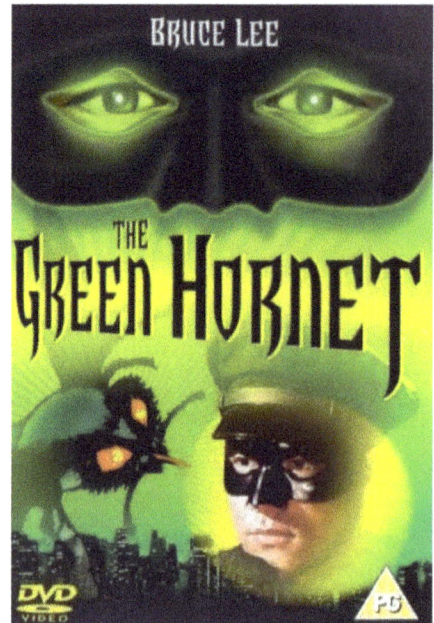

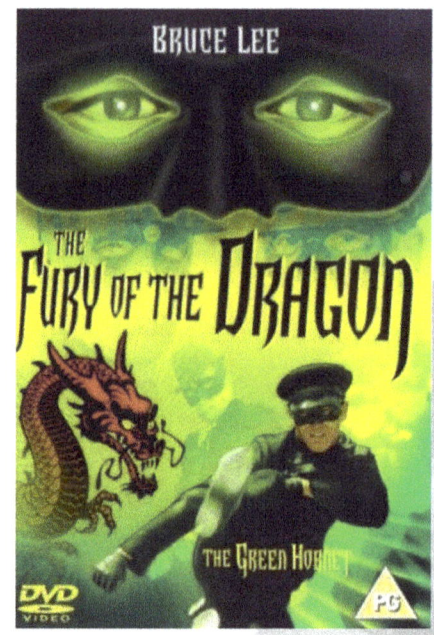

3) The 2011 Green Hornet Movie - Blu-ray Steelbook

Ok, ok, no Bruce Lee in this one at all, but I mention it partly as it may give us some insight into where the rights for the original show currently languish and partly as you can pick this up extremely cheaply. I rewatched the movie recently in preparation to write this article, and maybe it's a sign that my modern movie expectations have taken such a nose dive over the past few years given Hollywood's woefully bad output of late, but it was far better than I remembered.

Director Michel Gondry does a pretty decent job of retelling the Green Hornet origin tale and even manages to slip in a few of his trademark visual effects in here, most notably in his concept for 'Kato Vision' which riffs on a trick he used in his Music Video for the White Stripes song 'The Hardest Button to Button' wherein multiple versions of the same prop are used, here to help give the appearance of time expanding as Jay Chou's Kato appears to move so fast that time literally 'stretches' out around him. It's a pretty neat trick and one I've not seen anywhere else other than in Gondry's own videos. Seth Rogan co-wrote the screenplay and plays Britt Reid aka The Green Hornet himself. I can take or leave Rogan's comedy usually, but the excellent supporting cast assembled by Gondry around him does mostly manage to make up for his shortcomings.

The wonderful Christophe Waltz chewing up the scenery on villain duty as the impossible to remember 'Chudnofsky' and Blade Runner/ Battlestar Galactica veteran Edward James Olmos playing The long suffering Editor of the Newspaper that Rogan's inherits after his father's (Tom Wilkinson) death. For any Stranger Things fans out there we also have Sheriff Hopper himself, David Harbour here playing the D.A Scanlon.

But really this is a movie worth watching just for Jay Chou's more than presentable take on Kato and for the updated version of the Green Hornet's signature car, The Black Beauty.

If you can find this Steelbook edition of the movie, it comes housed in a rather nice case with the Black Beauty's Grill emblazoned on the front cover. There's a decent smattering of extra features on the disc, and when I last checked you can pick this up for less than the price of a Starbucks.

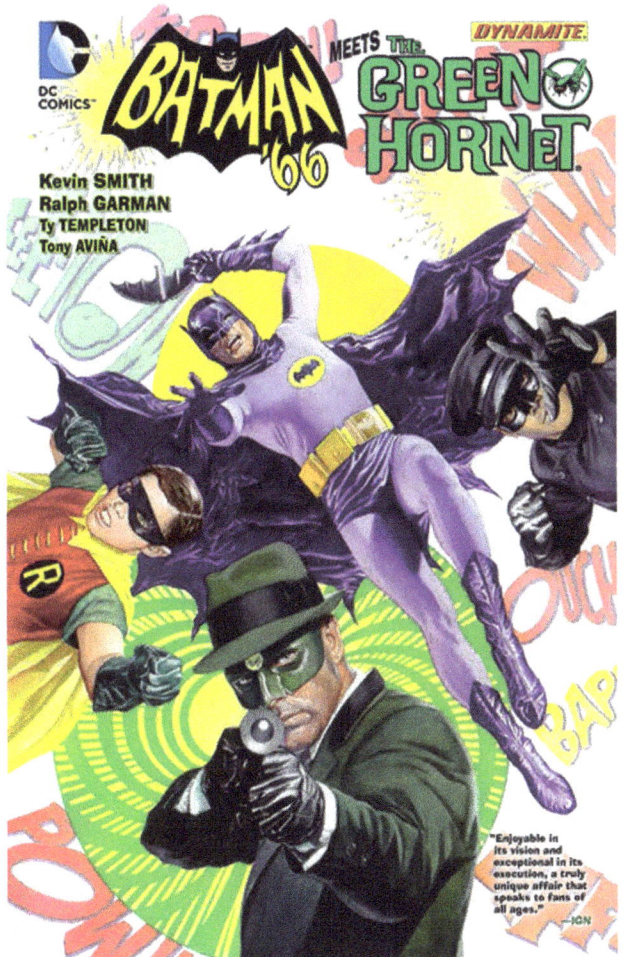

4) Batman 66 meets the Green Hornet Comic mini-series

The Writer/ Director/ Actor Kevin Smith tends to have a marmite effect on most folks these days, you either love him or hate him, but over the past few decades he has been steadily working away on various comic book titles, having written for Marvel, DC and Dynamite Comics (the current home of the Green Hornet) fairly regularly. He's been a pretty steady Batman writer but for me some of his best work can be found here, In his take on Batman 66 Meets the Green Hornet, originally a 6 part mini-series that built on Smith's extensive work on the Standalone Green Hornet comic, but by focusing on the TV incarnations of the characters, Smith really found the right tone to channel Adam West's The Caped Crusader well. The biggest selling point for this series for me though are the individual covers, drawn by Artist extraordinaire Alex Ross, if you can find the original 6 part run for a reasonable price, snap them up, as Ross's cover's are simply glorious.
DC also re-released the run in a Hard cover version and a Trade Paperback.
'Holy effective Crossover Batman.'

5) Green Hornet Action Figures (Various)

I would be remiss if I didn't draw your collective attention towards the HUGE amount of Bruce Lee as Kato and Green Hornet action figures that have been produced over the years.

There are far too many of these for me to round them up without this Blu-ray section of the magazine being taken over wholesale as an Action Figure section, But suffice to say there have been dozen's of different incarnations from various companies produced. Many of these now sell for pretty crazy amounts. I am no Action Figure collector, but those in the know inform me that one of the best of the bunch was produced by Enterbay, notable not just in that it was a standalone Kato figure (usually the figures come in bundled pairs of Hornet and Kato) but also in that the level of detail and likeness to Bruce Lee is particularly solid, and it's one of the more articulated figures available (seemingly that's a good thing) so much better served to position it in more credible poses for display. At the other end of the pricing spectrum, the frustratingly popular Funko Pop range also made a Green Hornet and Kato set, which look about as much like Bruce Lee and Van Williams as any Funko looks like its subject (which is not that much imho). You can pick up those if you're so inclined for about £10.

6) Dragon The Bruce Lee Story - Blu-ray and DVD

Lastly, it's worth also mentioning that there is one pretty short but fun sequence in the Jason Scott Lee starring Bruce Lee biopic directed by the original Fast and Furious director Rob Cohen which showcases Lee's hiring to play Kato by a fictional producer (played by Robert Wagner) and the subsequent filming of the pilot episode of the series.

The actor playing the Director of the show is Bruce Lee's real life co-star in the original 60's series.
The Green Hornet himself Van Williams. It's a pretty small part in the movie, and maybe not worth tracking down the film for just that, but the Blu-Ray is widely available, and has as many fans as it does detractors, personally, I don't mind it, Jason Scott Lee did his best and it's for the most part a very respectful and arguably hero-worshiping account of Lee's life.

With the considerable success of online petitions by fans to effect change on Hollywood over the past few years: Pushing Ryan Reynolds Deadpool project into production, forcing character redesigns on the live action Sonic the Hedgehog movie and maybe most famously of all, convincing DC and Warner Brothers to allow Zack Snyder to finish his original cut of his Justice League movie, the time may be right for an online campaign to call for the release of all 26 episodes of the 1960's Green Hornet show which introduced so many audiences to Bruce Lee for the first time. I for one would sign my name in agreement…

Written By Johnny Burnett AKA The Fanatical Dragon
https://www.youtube.com/c/TheFanaticalDragon

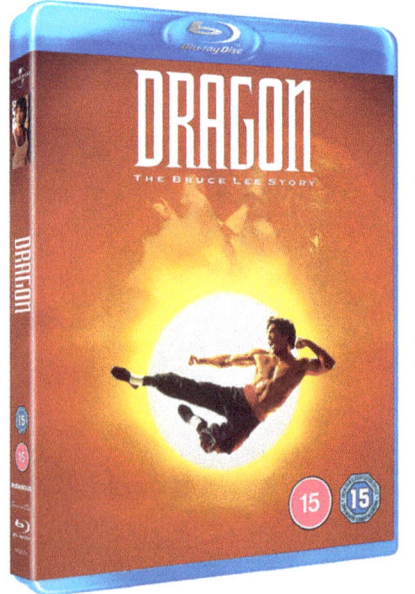

www.ingramcontent.com/pod-product-compliance
Lightning Source LLC
Chambersburg PA
CBHW051307110526

44589CB00025B/2969